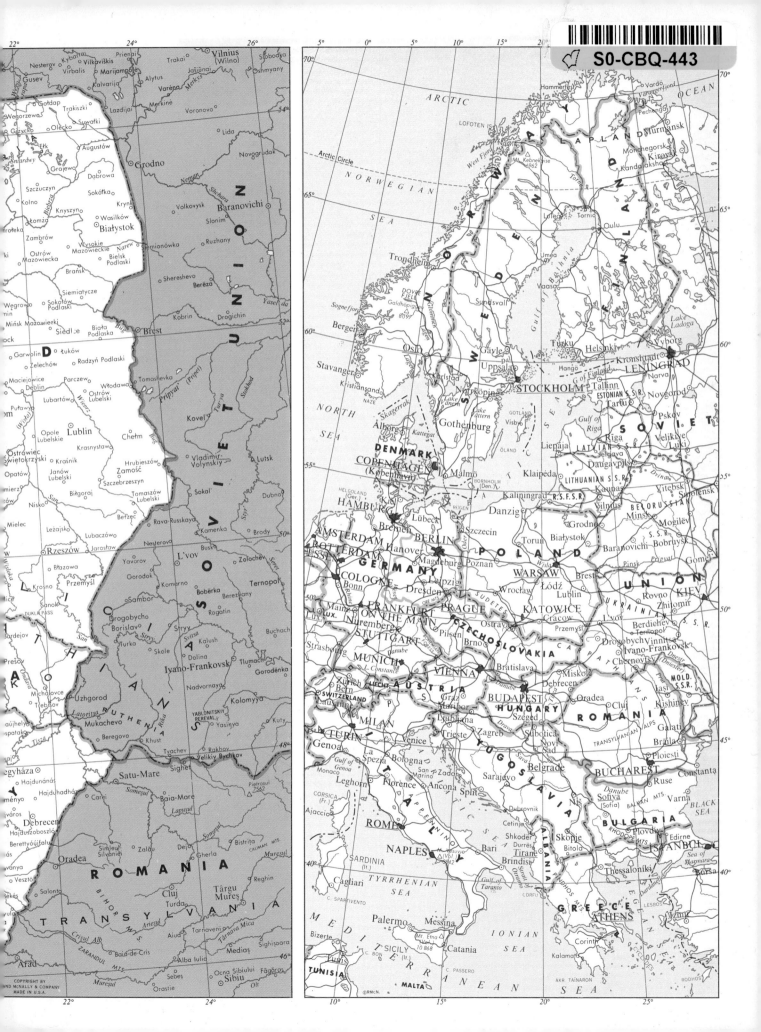

LIFE WORLD LIBRARY

EASTERN EUROPE

TIME
LIFE
BOOKS

LIFE World Library
LIFE Nature Library
LIFE Science Library
The LIFE History of the United States
Great Ages of Man
LIFE Pictorial Atlas of the World
The Epic of Man
The Wonders of Life on Earth
The World We Live In
The World's Great Religions
The LIFE Book of Christmas
LIFE's Picture History of Western Man
The LIFE Treasury of American Folklore
America's Arts and Skills
300 Years of American Painting
The Second World War
LIFE's Picture History of World War II
Picture Cook Book
LIFE Guide to Paris
TIME Reading Program

LIFE WORLD LIBRARY

EASTERN EUROPE

CZECHOSLOVAKIA, HUNGARY, POLAND

by Godfrey Blunden

and The Editors of LIFE

TIME INCORPORATED   NEW YORK

COVER: Graceful arcades of
Renaissance houses stretch along
the town square of Telč,
Czechoslovakia. The excellence
of the town's architecture
has prompted the Government
to name Telč a national monument.

ABOUT THE WRITER

Godfrey Blunden, author of the interpretive text for this volume in the LIFE
World Library, is a former associate editor of TIME who has been reporting
the international scene for many years. After working for various newspapers
in his native Australia, he became a war correspondent in the European theater
on the outbreak of World War II and was eventually assigned to Moscow. He
was among the few Western reporters to witness the Battle of Stalingrad and
the bitter fighting on the Kharkov and Rzhev fronts. Toward the conclusion
of the war he was attached to the U.S. Ninth Army and covered its meeting with
the Russian forces in Central Europe. After the war he served as a foreign correspondent for British Commonwealth newspapers. He joined TIME as a foreign-
news writer in 1950 and in 1958 became a correspondent for the TIME-LIFE News
Service in Paris. During his years with TIME he specialized in the affairs of Eastern
Europe, making annual trips to the region. Now an American citizen, he resigned
from the magazine in 1964 to work on a novel.

Contents

TIME-LIFE BOOKS

EDITOR
Norman P. Ross
TEXT DIRECTOR   ART DIRECTOR
William Jay Gold   Edward A. Hamilton
CHIEF OF RESEARCH
Beatrice T. Dobie
Assistant Text Director: Jerry Korn
Assistant Art Director: Arnold Holeywell
Assistant Chief of Research: Monica O. Horne

•

PUBLISHER
Rhett Austell
General Manager: Joseph C. Hazen Jr.
Business Manager: John D. McSweeney
Circulation Manager: Joan D. Manley

LIFE MAGAZINE

EDITOR: Edward K. Thompson
MANAGING EDITOR: George P. Hunt
PUBLISHER: Jerome S. Hardy

LIFE WORLD LIBRARY

SERIES EDITOR: Oliver E. Allen
Editorial Staff for *Eastern Europe:*
Assistant Editor: Jay Brennan
Designer: Ben Schultz
Chief Researcher: Grace Brynolson
Researchers: Jill Adams, Paula von Haimberger Arno, Irene Ertugrul,
Donald Newton, Madeleine Richards, Linda Wolfe

EDITORIAL PRODUCTION
Color Director: Robert L. Young
Art Assistants: James D. Smith, John M. Woods
Picture Researchers: Margaret K. Goldsmith, Joan Lynch
Copy Staff: Marian Gordon Goldman, Patricia Miller,
Dolores A. Littles

The text for the chapters of this book was written by Godfrey Blunden; the picture essays were written by George Constable. Many of the photographs were taken by Elliott Erwitt. Valuable help was also provided by the following individuals and departments of Time Incorporated: Margaret Bourke-White, Alfred Eisenstaedt and Michael Rougier, LIFE staff photographers; Doris O'Neil, Chief, LIFE Picture Library; Content Peckham, Chief, Time Inc. Bureau of Editorial Reference; and Richard M. Clurman, Chief, TIME-LIFE News Service.

Introduction

Eastern Europe is one of the most complex and tragic areas in the world. Inhabited by several peoples who speak a variety of languages and espouse different faiths, the region for centuries has been a fated borderland of empire, a thoroughfare of conquest, and an object of partition and subjection. Yet its several parts have maintained their identities and contributed their share to Western civilization from Copernicus and Hus to Chopin, Liszt and Bartók.

America's affinity with the troubled nations of Eastern Europe runs deep and strong. Polish patriots like Pułaski and Kościuszko joined our fight for national independence. We, in turn, became a rallying ground for the independence movements of Kossuth of Hungary, Masaryk of Czechoslovakia and Paderewski of Poland. Indeed, it was a President of the United States, Woodrow Wilson, who first proclaimed the complete restoration of a reunited, independent Poland as an incontrovertible aim of the Allies during World War I. The agreement that Czechs and Slovaks would unite to form a new country was signed at Pittsburgh, Pennsylvania, in 1918. Millions of our best citizens descend from those who sought "the bread of freedom" here when it was denied in Eastern Europe.

The fate of the peoples of Eastern Europe during and after World War II lays claim to our profound compassion. Brutal death factories, total reprisals and mass assassinations exterminated millions of Jews and decimated the remaining population in an incredible compendium of horror unrivaled throughout history. With peace came an alien ideology and the excesses of the Stalinist police state. Those dark years were followed in the later 1950s by the release of forces for change which, despite erratic progress and frequent disillusionment, have contributed to internal liberalization, a show of freer national expression and an opening of "windows to the West."

Beneath the drab and oppressive conformity of Communism, Eastern Europe today is undergoing a quiet evolution conditioned by the dynamics of reform within the Communist world and by that world's relations with the West. Another factor in this process is the alienation of most Eastern Europeans from things Russian.

The destalinization begun by Khrushchev unfroze a static situation and breached the barriers to change. It gathered momentum with the provocative examples of Communist but independent Yugoslavia, rebellious Hungary, revisionist Poland, defiant Albania and deviant Romania. The Sino-Soviet dispute powerfully adds to the element of flux in the region.

Perhaps most important is lagging economic development in the area, which places the regimes under growing pressures to orient economic planning along more rational lines and to open channels of trade and technical exchange with the West.

President Lyndon B. Johnson's policy of building "bridges of increased trade, of ideas, of visitors and of humanitarian aid" between East and West constitutes a positive and constructive approach to strengthening ties and broadening relations with Eastern Europe. While it would be too much to expect that our initiatives can rapidly modify the Eastern European reality, they do serve to illuminate and reinforce the community of interest between our country and that area.

This book affords Americans an opportunity to review in brief compass the background and highlights of current problems in Eastern Europe. The presentation is vivid and the subject most topical. Author Godfrey Blunden and the Editors of the Life World Library are to be congratulated on this addition to a notable series.

JACOB D. BEAM
former U.S. Ambassador to Poland

1

The Troubled Lands

THE traveler comes upon the scene with surprise and, perhaps, some disappointment: parallel fences, about six paces apart, made of concrete posts threaded with rusty barbed wire. The wire does not appear to be electrified, but the impression may be false. A young soldier with a submachine gun slung over his back leads a pair of farm horses harnessed to a set of harrows into the area between the fences; he mounts the plow and drives off. Every day this is done to keep the earth between the fences freshly turned so that the police dogs which lope up and down the passage can pick up the scent of anyone who has passed that way. That mines can be quickly planted in the loose earth is obvious.

Looking along the line of the fences, the traveler will see wooden watchtowers called miradors, from which armed sentries constantly survey the whole area. They do not hesitate to fire on strangers coming within rifle range of the fences, and many people have been killed this way.

This is a section of the Iron Curtain which for the last 20 years has bisected the continent of Europe, separating Poland, Czechoslovakia and Hungary from the Western Europe to which they are bound by historical and cultural ties. The Curtain varies in width and complexity according to the terrain; the mine fields, it is believed, are extensive in some places. There are also sectors where orthodox

9

military defenses stand behind the prison fences. Similar Iron Curtains also separate Poland, Czechoslovakia and Hungary from one another and from the Soviet Union.

In recent years, there has been a relaxation of the rules of exclusivity. The approved maps now show 11 places at which the foreigner may enter Czechoslovakia and Hungary from West Germany and Austria, and three points at which he may enter Poland after passing through East Germany. He can also pass between Poland and Czechoslovakia and Czechoslovakia and Hungary at more than a dozen spots on the frontiers. Some entry points are more in use than others. On a vacation weekend, for example, the visitor may find himself behind several busloads of young Americans and a mile-long file of West German automobiles waiting to enter Czechoslovakia from West Germany on the road leading to Pilsen and Prague. But mostly the traffic is commercial—trucks returning from the West or en route in the opposite direction with merchandise for sale. The first of two wooden booms is raised for each entering vehicle in turn and then lowered again, and there may be a wait of 10, perhaps 15, minutes during which passports and visas are examined. The traveler is asked to show what money he is carrying, and the amount is noted; when he leaves the territory some days or weeks later, this will be checked against his receipts for exchanged bills or traveler's checks. His automobile registration and insurance papers are studied, and his car is quickly, but expertly, searched. A lady's handbag may be swiftly weighed in the hand, the trunk of the car opened, suitcases searched, seats pulled up, the chassis rapidly glanced at.

THE security guards are not friendly. Implicit in the procedure is the possibility that the visitor may be personally searched, detained and interrogated. For the traveler who has never undergone the experience, it is a novel reminder—as the second boom is raised and the car is waved on—that henceforth, although his hard currency may be desirable, no habeas corpus protects him.

These are the loneliest roads in Europe. For scores of miles, except at the peak of the tourist season, a driver may encounter no other automobile. Those he does see will be of an unfamiliar make and design: Skodas, Tatras, Warszawas and Syrenas. Gas stations will be few and far between, and except at the rare, special tourist pumps, the gas they dispense is too crude for foreign carburetors; the smell of low-octane gas will haunt the visitor everywhere. There are policemen patrolling the highways, but if one's car breaks down on the road they are unlikely to help. Main roads are poorly marked and side roads not at all. Drivers cannot be certain that rough spots and washouts will be indicated. On the long stretches of cobblestone roads tires will roar. At railroad crossings the gates come down 10 minutes before a train appears; children stare at the steam locomotive. In the loneliest places the visitor will pass people walking along, always carrying something. Eastern Europe is not yet on wheels, but this is the visitor's gain: no parking problems, no traffic noise in a city hotel and nothing to mar the sound of birds at dawn.

HE will see some wonderfully varied country: forests of speckled birches, firs like those of Oregon, oak woods, mile-wide swaths of grainfields, fallow land, rocky heights, mirage-veiled plains, two or three very ancient and beautiful towns, four or five ugly but fascinating cities. In Poland, there are thousands of lakes, as well as yellow Baltic beaches edged with pinewoods; in Czechoslovakia, hilltop castles, underground caverns and famous old spas; in Hungary, hot mineral springs, old citadels, vineyards and the noble Danube. Any sportsman will see that there is game all over this part of Europe: stags, wolves, wild boars, almost every kind of field and water fowl, and even bears. The bears, incidentally, are the only creatures of any size that ignore the strict border regulations with impunity. In the High Tatra, on the border between Poland and Czechoslovakia, a colony of about 14 of them moves from one side of the mountain to the other, from Poland to Czechoslovakia and back again, winter and summer, climbing over the man-made barriers, ignored by the guards.

The foreign visitor will come upon huge industrial centers; the landscape of coke ovens and blast furnaces will be familiar to him, but the names will not be. He will see many shabby housing developments

MAJOR REGIONS in Eastern Europe are shown in black type on the map at right. Many of them, like Bohemia, Silesia and Galicia, were originally small kingdoms or duchies; others, like Moravia and Pomerania, were crown lands or principalities. In an area in which national frontiers have changed so frequently, the regions retain an individual importance. Many of them in fact overlap today's borders between countries. Languages and physical differences vary from one region to another even within the same country.

and poorly dressed people. After the show-window perfection of West Germany the villages and houses will seem neglected and in need of repairs and paint. He will see the black rubble of World War II still lying here and there. Everywhere he will see women doing men's work, as they have for generations, working in the fields, driving tractors, trucks and streetcars. Yet, if the visitor is privately entertained, he will observe men bowing to ladies and to one another, kissing ladies' hands and maintaining the old, polite forms of address, especially in Poland and Hungary. He will see some handsome women, but he may be puzzled by their hat styles until he realizes that fashions are dictated by what is available from state-run factories. A hat, of course, is a sign of superior status; most women wear babushkas. He will see television antennas everywhere, but he will miss seeing or hearing what he has always thought

of as news. He will be struck by the absence of commercial advertising, printed or uttered, and as a result his eye will become especially aware of the rare posters erected by state tourist offices suggesting vacations in what to him are unfamiliar places—in the Russian Caucasus, for example. The visitor will notice that most of his fellow tourists are Russians, and he will be able to judge the drabness of their existence at home by their exclamations of pleasure in present surroundings. He will soon note that night life comes to a halt once the theaters have emptied and that the city streets are so dimly lighted that some people find their way home with the aid of flashlights.

Eastern Europe is indeed dark and drab. The explanation is not hard to find; it is forced upon the observer by the repeated evidence of wrecked towns, battle cemeteries, modest memorials to uncounted

11

massacres and destruction, and the vestiges of World War II concentration camps. No friendly purse has been opened for the reparation of intolerable experiences; on the contrary, it would seem that the lords of these lands would have the people's memory shaped in the matrix of defeat.

They are not, however, a people easily daunted. More than 1,000 years of recorded history lie behind Poland, Hungary and Czechoslovakia. The names of the countries are relatively new; their present governments, imposing an altered style of life, are even newer. For them, upheavals are not unusual. The three nations, lying in a great wedge between Russia and Germany, have been recurrently subject to the demographic and martial pressures of their two powerful neighbors—and to the interference of others as well. Partition agreements concluded between the great powers of Europe from 1772 to 1795, at the Congress of Vienna in 1815 and at the Paris Peace Conference in 1919 brought about vast changes in the region's national borders and in the political structures of the three countries—and so, inevitably, did the meetings of the American, British and Russian chiefs of state at Yalta and Potsdam in 1945. Victorious in World War II, the Soviet Union demanded and, with the assent of its Western allies, obtained hegemony over Poland, Czechoslovakia and Hungary. The new governments of the three countries were eventually supplanted by Communist-controlled regimes—which were, in turn, subject to the control of the Soviet Union. The frontiers of Poland were shifted westward at the end of the war while the Soviet Union incorporated 69,400 square miles of eastern Poland within its own borders; Czechoslovakia lost to the Soviet Union its eastern province, Ruthenia, which gave Russia a common frontier with Hungary.

The people were in no position to protest. Poland's economy, for example, had been immeasurably

A GUIDE TO PLACE NAMES

The troubled history of Eastern Europe and its involved patterns of migration, settlement and conquest have left the region with many place names that have more than one form. In general this book uses local place names. In some cases it employs names that have come to be commonly accepted in English: "Prague," for example, rather than the Czech "Praha." This rule has been followed even when the name has come into English usage from a language other than that of the country within whose borders the place now lies. "Danzig," for example, is derived from German; the Poles themselves refer to the city as "Gdánsk."

damaged in the war, and more than 15 per cent of its population had perished. Czechoslovakia's and Hungary's losses were comparatively less, but still great for countries of their size: 500,000 Hungarians and 250,000 Czechoslovaks died during the war; property damage in the two nations amounted to an estimated $15 billion. At the end of the war 13 to 14 million people—Germans, Poles, Hungarians and Slovaks—had been rooted out of homes their families had occupied in the three countries for generations, some of them expropriated down to their last shirts and sent to find new homes hundreds of miles distant. Moreover, some four to five million former inhabitants were straggling back from prison camps and rehabilitation centers all over Europe and Asia. By the time the refugees had settled down it was evident that the Communist leaders, isolating these countries from the West and dominating the intellectual and spiritual lives of the inhabitants, had embarked upon a process of sovietization which was leading toward virtual annexation. Protests were stifled, and dissidence within the Communist Parties was crushed by classic Soviet methods of repression. Eastern Europe was stagnating when, in 1956, there were spontaneous uprisings against Communist rule in Poland and Hungary. Although ruthlessly crushed, these revolts have had a profound effect on subsequent Soviet policies—and manifestations of the spirit of revolt can still be seen everywhere in the region.

The Student Satirical Theater in Warsaw has a popular skit which shows an encounter between a contemporary young man and a middle-aged gentleman who has just emerged from a nearby wood with a basket of mushrooms. It transpires that the middle-aged man entered the wood in September 1939 and has been lost there ever since. The young man begins to enlighten him on what has happened in Poland in the ensuing years. The mushroom gatherer is incredulous. Then as the young man goes on to talk with a certain blandness about the commonplaces of modern Poland, the mushroom gatherer becomes increasingly upset. "But it's all right," the young man assures him. "It's really all right." Now plainly alarmed, the mushroom gatherer says goodbye, picks up his basket and goes back into the wood. "Wait a minute," says the young man, "I'm coming with you." As he goes off stage he winks solemnly at the audience. "I have to convince him," he says.

The skit about the mushroom gatherer never fails to provoke laughter. There is something indomitable about people who take their troubles this way.

Who are they? What are they like, these 55 million people who live in Poland, Czechoslovakia and Hungary? Perhaps the simplest way to differentiate the three peoples is to observe that the Poles are vodka drinkers, the Czechs beer drinkers and the Hungarians wine drinkers. The respective beverages are produced in the three countries for geographic reasons: Hungary, for example, has many sunny hillsides for the cultivation of grapes; Czechoslovakia possesses excellent water and fine hops; grains and potatoes, out of which vodka is made, grow well on the Polish plain. But the popularity of the drinks in their native countries also says something about the customs and character of the different peoples. The Poles are a moody people who take their fiery vodka in one violent gulp; the Czechs, like the neighboring Germans, delight in jamming themselves into smoky beer halls to drink steins of beer and sing songs; the Hungarians feel happier with their fingers curled around a glass of golden Tokay.

All three peoples are frequently classified by foreigners as romantics, a characterization which perhaps means that through many centuries Eastern Europeans appear to have striven for the unreal, or at least the unrealizable: national independence. They

---

A GUIDE TO PRONUNCIATION

There are four major languages spoken in Eastern Europe: Hungarian, Polish, Czech and Slovak. The last two are so closely related that they are mutually intelligible. All of them offer difficulty to speakers of English. Many consonants and all the vowels vary in pronunciation, and each language uses a variety of diacritical marks. For most proper names in this book native spellings are used, and a few pronunciation hints are offered here. In Polish the acute accent (´) makes "s" sound like "sh." Polish also has a specially marked letter ("ł") which makes Władysław Gomułka's name sound like "Vooadysooav Gomuooka." In Czech the haček (ˇ) turns "s," "c," "z" and "r" into "sh," "tsh," "zh" and "rzh," as in Beneš (Benesh) or Dvořák (Dvorzhak). In Hungarian "cs" is "tch" and "s" is "sh," as in *csárdás*, the dance, which is pronounced *tchardash*.

---

are certainly brave enough. Polish intrepidity, for example, is legendary. In his classic novel *War and Peace* Leo Tolstoy tells of Napoleon's ordering a regiment of Polish cavalry to cross a river. Instead of riding to a nearby, safe ford, the Poles plunge into the swift river, losing a number of horses and men. During World War II Polish squadrons of the British Royal Air Force flew more sorties and suffered more casualties than almost any others.

All Hungary throbs with the romance of revolutions long past and near present. Just before his death in 1937 Thomas Masaryk, who founded the first Czechoslovak republic after years of struggle, wrote: "Perhaps in fifty years our times will appear to people living then in such a haze of splendor that they will almost envy us." The Poles and the Hungarians have a sense of style in dress; they are proud soldiers and farmers; their native music and dancing are full of verve. The Czechs are more phlegmatic; they are the better administrators and more skilled engineers. All three peoples have an intense sense of belonging to those particular plains, mountains and valleys where they and their ancestors have lived for so many centuries. Oddly enough, although their histories have been similar in many respects, they are not particularly fond of one another.

The overwhelming majority of the Poles and the Czechoslovaks are Slavs, and they constitute about one fourth of the Slav population of the world. No one quite knows how or where the Slavs originated. In prehistoric times they apparently settled in what is now western Russia and eastern Poland. They lived in circular or horseshoe-shaped villages composed of log huts sunk into the ground, and were animists whose gods were the sun and the elements. They cultivated the soil with forked sticks, raised cattle, sheep and goats, and hunted. They first appear in recorded history in the First Century A.D., when Roman writers reported that they lived along the Vistula River in what is now Poland.

In those ancient times the Central Asian steppe was an inexhaustible reservoir of nomadic tribes which emerged from the east to plunder more fruitful and settled areas. Recurrent waves of these invaders kept Eastern Europe's population in a state of flux for long periods. Eventually the Slav settlers along the Vistula were dispersed. In the dark centuries which followed the barbarians' seizure of Rome the Slavs migrated—although their movements are obscure. When the curtain went up on the Middle Ages they had traveled west and were settled on the rivers Elbe and Saale in what is now Germany; they had circled eastward through Kiev and reached the Don in modern Russia; they had crossed the Danube and were settled along the rivers Drava and Sava in modern Croatia and southern Hungary; they had moved south down the Adriatic coast, threatened Greece and actually reached as far south as Crete. Without attracting much notice they had moved slowly in island-communities, threading their way through other barbarian groups.

When finally settled, they gradually became differentiated from one another. Thus the author of an 11th Century Russian chronicle records: "Some came and settled by the river Morava and were called Moravians, while others were called Czechs. Among these same Slavs are included the White Croats, the Serbs and the Carinthians. . . ." Elsewhere the Slav peoples also came to be known by geographic terms. Those who lived on the *po-more,* or "seacoast," for example, were called Pomeranians, and those who lived in the *pole,* or "open country," were known as Polyanians.

LACKING political unity, the Slavs were subject to the continued harassment of the Asian hordes. A Turko-Tatar tribe called the Bulgars held the Slavs in fief for a time, but in the Seventh Century were themselves diverted into the southern regions of Europe now known as the Balkans by new arrivals known as the Avars. A tribe of horsemen from Central Asia, the Avars had crossed the steppe and, occupying the lands of the Danube, proceeded to extract brutal tribute from the peoples of Eastern Europe. Samo, a merchant, united the Czechs against

them, the first known instance of a union of Slavs.

With the successive invasions the physical characteristics that had formerly distinguished the Slavs —a long "northern" head and blond hair—gave way to the round head and dark hair of the typical middle European of today. The term "Slav" is believed to have been first used in a Sixth Century Greek text. Some Slav philologists believe that it derives from the Slav word for glory *(slava).* Other philological experts claim that it derives from the word for speech *(slovo).* However, as an outcome of the nearly universal practice of raiding the populous Slav communities to carry off the young, the word "Slav" was adopted into every European language in another sense: *Sklave* (German), *slaaf* (Dutch), *esclave* (French)—all of them meaning "slave." As one historian has said: "The Slavs, as pagans, were beyond the pale of humanity, and when captured were sold like cattle."

THE Magyars were among the Eastern peoples who supplied themselves with Slav prisoners. A dark-haired people from Central Asia, the Magyars had established themselves on the Don River early in the Christian era. Horsemen whose main diet was meat, fish and mare's milk, they came to be known as the On Ogurs, or "the people of 10 arrows." In the Ninth Century the On Ogurs were driven west from the Don. They crossed the Carpathian Mountains and settled in the Danube basin, overwhelming the Slavs of the area. Thenceforward the On Ogurs made the Danube plain their home.

By 907 they had extended their sovereignty as far as the river Enns in present-day Austria. For decades they were the scourge of Europe. Wearing shirts of mail and plumed helmets, riding fast horses and fighting from the saddle, they sortied as far as Orléans, Nîmes, Bremen and Constantinople, looting churches and collecting slaves. The cry "On Ogur-r-r!" struck terror into every European breast. But they were eventually to become a settled Christian people. The force which tamed the On Ogurs, and in effect caused the dread words "On Ogur" to become the peaceful word "Hungarian," was the same force which was also to bring the Slavs into the Western Christian community: the extending influence of the new Holy Roman Empire.

A girl smiles from a streetcar rumbling through Cracow, Poland. In the left background is the 600-year-old Dominican Church.

Tradition Surviving in a Rigorous New Order

The evidences of Eastern Europe's long, full history are an ever-present background to the new order of Communism. The peasants tilling huge collective farms still dress and live as they did when they worked for great landowners. Villages and cities are studded with edifices many centuries old. Amidst the slogan-bolstered bustle of the cities, old habits persist; people continue to love fine manners. The young, however, have developed—as elsewhere in the world—a fondness for styles other than those of their elders. In the large cities the mode of dress and the dances are only a step behind those of the West.

VILLAGE WAYS *have changed little, despite social and economic revolutions*

PUSHING A CART into their village at the end of the day, peasants bring home a harvest of grapes in the Little Carpathian mountain region, an area in southwest Czechoslovakia known for wine making.

PLAYING CARDS, farmers pass the time *(left)* in a small town in northern Hungary. The game is *ultimó,* which is like whist or bridge; it has long been a favorite gambling game among Hungarians of all classes.

LEAVING CHURCH, Hungarian women *(opposite)* pause to chat in the sun after Mass. This village church near Gyöngyös dates back to the 15th Century. Seven out of 10 Hungarians are Roman Catholics.

TALL SHADE TREES line a road traveled by two Polish children *(above)* as livestock graze in the background. Despite recent industrializing efforts, Poland retains a largely rural look.

WEATHER-SCARRED STATUES overshadow three children hiking into a central Czechoslovakian town. Dating from the 16th Century, the statues honor Moravian saints and heroes.

BRILLIANT COSTUMES are worn by women *(below)* out for a Sunday walk in Boldog, Hungary. Such traditional outfits are seen in almost every Hungarian village on Sundays and holidays.

A YOUNG FARMER examines the green grapes he has harvested near the Czechoslovakian town of Modra, in the Little Carpathian Mountains. Modra is the site of a wine-making school.

SMALL PLEASURES and ancient customs hold their own everywhere in the regimented and fast-paced cities

A WEDDING PARTY poses for a picture in front of the 600-year-old Town Hall in Old Town Square, Prague. Neighboring buildings in the square are festooned with Communist banners.

CROWDED SHOPPERS examine produce at stalls in Budapest's Great Market Hall *(right)*. Private stalls are allowed to compete with publicly owned groceries, but their prices are higher.

TWO MOTORCYCLISTS fill up on gas in Pécs, Hungary. Hungary has few automobiles and poor roads; even motorcycle riding is largely confined to the cities and surrounding areas.

WELL-MANNERED BUSINESSMAN greets a friend *(below)* as workers hurry through Market Square in Cracow, Poland. The square has changed little since it was originally laid out in 1275.

A VARIED NIGHT LIFE *continues to flourish in sophisticated urban cities*

PRAGUE PERFORMERS enact *King Ubu*, a drama attacking bourgeois values by the 19th Century French playwright Alfred Jarry. A remarkable number of plays —many of them translated foreign works —are produced in Prague's 22 theaters.

GLITTERING RESTAURANT resplendent with gilt balustrades reflects Budapest's flair for elegance *(opposite)*. Called the Hungaria, the restaurant was long a meeting place for theater people and journalists; today it caters to the family trade.

STARK PANTOMIME called *The Bump* is performed in an experimental theater in Bratislava, Czechoslovakia. Theaters are not confined to the major cities: many small towns have their own. The Czechs are also great devotees of opera and ballet.

THE ENERGY OF YOUTH is expressed in Western-style dancing, music groups and earnest discussions

ROCK 'N' ROLL SINGERS, accompanied by an amateur music group composed of students and workers, rehearse their numbers in the 16th Century Old Baroque Music Hall in Prague.

UNIVERSITY STUDENTS chat *(above)* at a Warsaw club. One *(center)* wears a button of the Campaign for Nuclear Disarmament, which opposes all atomic testing.

YOUNG ACTORS from a Bratislava, Czechoslovakia, theater gather *(below)* at a restaurant after a show. Paid from box-office receipts, they earn up to $28 a week.

PARTYGOERS dance at the Cracow University Students' Club. Jazz and American dance fads have been immensely popular with the youths of Polish cities since the middle of the 1950s.

The sculpted head of King Casimir the Great, last ruler of Poland's original dynasty, the Piast, adorns his tomb in the Wawel Cathedral

in Cracow. Casimir founded the nation's first university in 1364.

2

Centuries of Growth and Struggle

"THERE were no nations in the 9th Century," the Belgian historian Henri Pirenne has noted. "There was only Christendom." Eastern Europe had long been ravaged by successive waves of pagan invaders. But in the year 796 Charlemagne, ruler of the Kingdom of the Franks, took his armies to the east and crushed the Avars, the most troublesome of these invaders. In Rome four years later Pope Leo III crowned Charlemagne Emperor of the Holy Roman Empire, that supposed rebirth of the power of the universal empire of Rome. The word "Holy" in the title was significant; the new Empire was to be firmly allied with the "One, Holy, Catholic and Apostolic" Roman Church. It did not take the pagan princes of Eastern Europe long to understand that embracing the Christian faith of the Holy Roman Empire made them part of something bigger than themselves, from which their petty dynasties would gain prestige and protection. Roman Catholicism, too, was to benefit substantially, for with the conversion of the ruler went the conversion of his people. Even before Charlemagne's assumption of the

27

imperial title, Christian missionaries had entered the Slav lands. Among the most important of them were Greek monks representing the Orthodox Eastern Church, which owed no allegiance to the Bishop of Rome. The Eastern missionaries were successful in Christianizing Moravia, a small principality in what is present-day Czechoslovakia. The country was soon to become Roman Catholic, however, for the region lay considerably closer to the sphere of influence of the Roman Catholic Holy Roman Empire than to that of Byzantium, center of Orthodoxy, and the Eastern Church gradually withdrew to the Balkans and to the Ukraine, or Kievan Russia as it was then called.

THE Roman Church had equal success elsewhere in Eastern Europe. In 895 the ruler of Bohemia, a small principality lying to the west of Moravia, declared himself a vassal of the Catholic Holy Roman Emperor, and the Slavs of Bohemia, known as the Czechs, were consequently converted to Catholicism. Only 70 years later, in 965, the Polish Prince Mieszko I married a Czech princess who had become a Catholic; he himself was converted and toward the end of his reign symbolically donated Poland to the Holy See. Roman Catholicism spread throughout his domain. As a result of Mieszko's conversion a Roman Catholic archbishopric was established in the year 1000 in Gniezno, Poland, and bishoprics were created in distant areas of the country. Poland, however, was the eastern frontier of Rome; beyond it Orthodoxy reigned.

Thus the Slavs as a whole were divided at an early date, those of Poland, Moravia and Bohemia embracing the Roman faith, those of the Balkans and Kievan Russia accepting the Orthodox. It was a broad and important division—between Eastern and Western Christianity, between Byzantium and Rome, between a culture conditioned by Greek and Levantine influence and one affected by the Teutonic spirit of the Holy Roman Empire, whose crown, after the death of Charlemagne, came increasingly to be settled on Germanic heads. The demarcation line between the two cultures would be the cause of ceaseless conflict in ensuing centuries, and the fluctuating vigor of the parent Churches and their royal allies would profoundly affect the character and institutions of the divided Slavs. In both Kievan Russia and Eastern Europe the long-term outcome would be the slow development of concepts of national identity among the Slav peoples and long and bitter struggles to establish nationhood.

The Magyars of Hungary were not, of course, members of the Slav family, but having settled in the middle Danube basin they too were affected by the forces which touched their Slav neighbors. The Hungarians at first lived in a society of independent clans, of which the Arpád family was the acknowledged, but not always the unchallenged, leader.

After the Arpád chief Géza was converted to Roman Catholicism in 973, great missionary activity set in and cordial relations were established with the Holy Roman Empire. Géza's son and successor, Stephen, married the sister of the Holy Roman Emperor, and appealed to Rome for recognition as king of Hungary. Legend says that Pope Sylvester presented Stephen with a golden crown and an Apostolic cross. Stephen's coronation on Christmas Day in the year 1000 marked the culmination of the fashioning of a medieval state out of the ancient Magyar clan system.

IN the brief span of two centuries—from 800 to 1000—Eastern Europe was thus swiftly Christianized. The ensuing spiritual and cultural benefits were incalculable. The political advantages were no less valuable. Eastern Europe's conversion imposed a certain restraint on the casual depredations of Western neighbors who had hitherto considered the pagan Slavs fair game. Yet there were disadvantages as well: wherever German missionary efforts reached, there was German colonization—and this, too, was to have far-reaching effects on Eastern Europe. In the 10th Century, Bohemia had carried on an intense struggle for survival against the pressure of the Germans to the north and west and the Magyars to the east and south. Prince Václav, of the Czech ruling family, the Přemyslids, was the first to recognize the futility of resistance, and before his death in 929 he acknowledged the overlordship of the Holy Roman Emperor. In Hungary, after the death of Stephen, there was an influx of Saxons and Germans, as well as Croats and Jews, and the country, increasing in size and population, gradually came to lack cohesive rule.

There were other troubles to come. In 1241 the Tatars, barbaric invaders from the Russian steppe, put eastern Bohemia to the torch after defeating the Russian and Polish armies, and, turning on Hungary, ravaged the countryside from end to end, killing half the inhabitants.

Yet, despite this disaster, Eastern Europe was not to slip back into the twilight of history. The old Árpád line became extinct in Hungary in 1301, and with the Pope's support the French Angevin family took over the monarchy; Hungary, under King Charles Robert and his son Louis the Great, entered on a period of stability. In Bohemia John of Luxembourg was elected King, and in 1346 the accession to the Bohemian throne of his son Charles IV, the Holy Roman Emperor, ushered in Bohemia's so-called "Golden Age."

THE flourishing silver mines at Kutná Hora made it possible to reform Bohemia's monetary system, and the Prague groat, a silver coin, became universal currency throughout Europe. Material and cultural progress went hand in hand. The first literary efforts in the local tongue had consisted of religious chants, prayers and stories of the native saints. From these had come simple secular songs like the Czech *"Hospodine Pomiluj"* (Lord Have Mercy upon Us). Prose works recounting the achievements of the ancient kings also appeared. The culmination of these cultural developments was the founding of the University of Prague in 1348.

Similarly in Hungary the mines of Transylvania, producing 3,000 pounds of gold a year, enabled King Charles Robert to introduce a systematic fiscal policy. At the same time a parallel literary development produced a comprehensive National Chronicle, one of the most magnificent illuminated works of the Middle Ages.

Poland, too, flourished in this period. Under Casimir III, the only Polish King to be designated "the Great," the country prospered economically, frontier defenses were improved, and Polish law was codified. The country was opened to Jewish refugees fleeing persecution in other lands. The University of Cracow was founded in 1364, and it produced a number of eminent scholars and stimulated the rise of a native literature.

In the midst of these affirmations of a dawning national consciousness, the constant pressure from the Germans, known as the *Drang nach Osten,* or "drive to the east," caused continuing concern. The chief threat came from the Teutonic Knights, a military and militant religious order which had been founded in Palestine in the 12th Century. The Teutonic Knights were a disciplined group of men, mostly of German origin, and they constituted one of the most powerful military organizations of the Middle Ages. Invited by the Poles in 1226 to help them secure additional territory by subduing the pagan tribes in what later became Prussia, the Knights had occupied the region and set about Germanizing the Prussians. No secret was made by the Knights of their intention to found an independent German state on the southern littoral of the Baltic Sea.

Eastern Europe responded to this expansionist threat by establishing a system of dynastic alliances. Casimir III was the last male of the old Piast line of Polish rulers. Before his death in 1370 he designated his nephew King Louis of Hungary to succeed him as King of Poland, but Louis had no male heirs either. In return for the grant of a charter of liberties to the Polish nobles, he asked them to name his daughter Mary as his successor. The nobles, however, were of no mind for continued Hungarian rule. When Louis died in 1382 they brought his 10-year-old daughter, Jadwiga, to Cracow, crowned her "King" and struck a bargain with Grand Duke Jagiełło of Lithuania. At this time Lithuania was a large, pagan country northeast of Poland. It shared Poland's apprehensions about the aims of the Teutonic Knights in the Baltic area. Jagiełło was baptized in 1386, and married Jadwiga in return for the Polish crown. The territories of the two countries were joined.

JAGIELLO'S baptism, in turn, led to the Christianizing of Lithuania, and the union of his land with Jadwiga's vastly added to the Polish domain, for Lithuania also included White Russia and much of the Ukraine. Thus the influence of Western Christian civilization was extended hundreds of miles to the east, to include the important centers of Wilno and Kiev.

Poles and Lithuanians then joined forces, and the Teutonic Knights were defeated in 1410 at the Battle

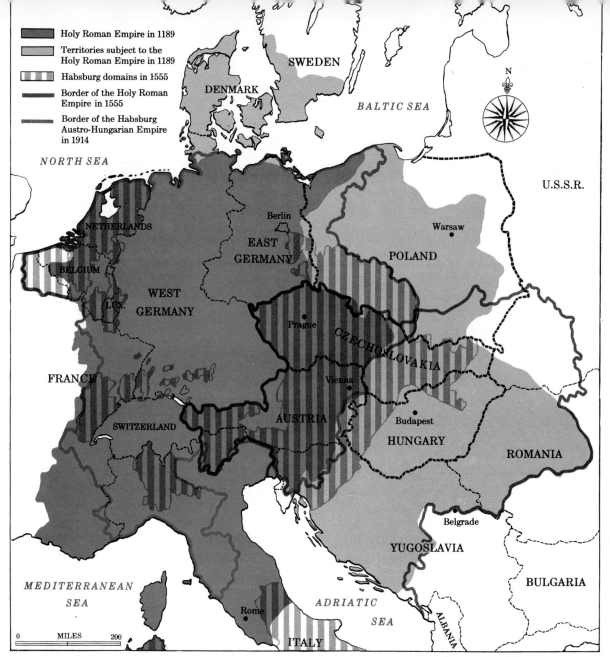

Legend

- Holy Roman Empire in 1189
- Territories subject to the Holy Roman Empire in 1189
- Habsburg domains in 1555
- Border of the Holy Roman Empire in 1555
- Border of the Habsburg Austro-Hungarian Empire in 1914

GERMANIC INFLUENCE in Eastern Europe is indicated by the map above, which shows the extent of the Holy Roman Empire and of the holdings of the Habsburg rulers of Austria at various stages in history. Originally centered on Germany and Italy, the Empire grew, under a succession of Germanic emperors, to include much of Europe. The emperors' powers fluctuated over the years, but the divided peoples of Eastern Europe were particularly vulnerable to their pressures. In 1438 the imperial title fell permanently to the Habsburgs. Through dynastic alliances they gained ever-increasing amounts of territory in the East. The Holy Roman Empire was dissolved in 1806, but the Habsburgs remained rulers of the Austro-Hungarian Empire until 1918.

of Grunwald (which was called Tannenberg by the Germans). The battle was one of the major turning points of European history: although the threat of Germanic expansion was by no means erased, the power of the Teutonic Knights was destroyed, and their dream of establishing a Germanic East European empire was shattered.

After Jagiełło died, his vast domain descended in 1447 to his youngest son, Casimir IV, who ruled the Polish-Lithuanian state for a period of 45 years. By pursuing a friendly policy toward Bohemia and Hungary, Casimir managed to secure the election of his eldest son, Ladislas, to the thrones of both of those countries as well. While Christopher Columbus was discovering the New World the Jagiełłonian dynasty was at the peak of its power: it ruled the entire area that is the subject of this book and far beyond it to the east.

Under the Jagiełłonians, who ruled until 1572, Poland was one of the most advanced countries in Europe. The nobility and gentry were granted the right of habeas corpus in 1430, and a parliament called the Sejm was formed in 1454. A peace treaty was signed with the Teutonic Knights in 1466. Sigismund I, who reigned from 1506 to 1548 and became known as "Poland's first modern ruler," married an Italian princess, who brought the art, architecture and ideas of the Italian Renaissance to her court in Cracow. There was a renewed interest in the Polish language, and the country produced its first great prose writer, Mikołaj Rej. Regarded as the father of Polish literature, he emphasized that the Poles, too, possessed and must employ their own language, and he was the first to write exclusively in Polish.

THE man who lastingly characterizes this period is Nicholas Copernicus, the son of a Polish merchant, who was born at Toruń in 1473. At the University of Cracow, then famous for its mathematics and astronomy, he discovered several contradictions in the system then used for calculating the movements of celestial bodies. Continuing his studies at the University of Bologna in Italy, he advanced the theory that the moon was a satellite of the earth. He studied law and medicine at Padua and took a doctorate in canon, or Church, law at Ferrara, also in Italy. As an official of the Cathedral of Frauenburg in northern Poland, he led a busy administrative life which included the organization of armed resistance against provocations by neighboring Teutonic Knights. At the same time he continued his astronomical studies and arrived at the conclusion that the earth was in orbit around the sun—a somewhat frightening idea, because it ran counter to the prejudice of the age, which held that the earth was the center of the universe. After countless observations he proved the theory in a paper which he circulated only among friends.

Further observation and experiment revealed to Copernicus that the mechanism of celestial motions was even more complicated than he had first thought. He discovered, for example, that the orbit of the earth around the sun had a variable eccentricity and that the sun itself was in motion toward the apparently fixed stars. In 1515 he began writing his great work, *De Revolutionibus Orbium Coelestium*. He did not dare to publish his findings immediately, being, as he wrote, "afraid of contempt brought about by the novelty and inconceivableness" of his new theory. But eventually he did publish the book, dedicating it to Pope Paul III. He died on May 24, 1543, a few hours after the arrival of the first printed copy of *De Revolutionibus* at his home in Frauenburg. The Pole who removed the earth from a standstill at the center of the universe made the world leap forward.

It is sometimes difficult for us to understand the importance of issues which disturbed people 500 years ago. Europe was emerging from ages of superstition toward the age of knowledge and enlightenment typified by Copernicus. The Church of Rome, which had won so many great spiritual victories in past centuries, was itself torn with internal dissension and worldly politics. From 1378 to 1417, there was in fact a "Great Schism," or split, during which there were two rival Popes. In the 16th Century the movement which aimed at the reformation of the doctrines and practices of the Church of Rome was to bring about the establishment of the various Reformed, or Protestant, Churches of Central and Northwestern Europe.

IN Eastern Europe the Czechs of Bohemia were among the first to be affected by the profound question of Church reform. The reasons "ran deep," as the American historian S. Harrison Thomson has written, and they were not solely religious, for they involved "social, economic and nationalistic elements as well." More than a century before Martin Luther precipitated the Protestant Reformation by nailing his 95 theses to the door of a church in Wittenberg, Germany, the Czech clergy had preached against the abuses Luther attacked: the sale of indulgences and Church positions, the excessive veneration of holy pictures and statues, and other evils.

One of the most outspoken advocates of Church reform at this time was Master John Hus, a priest and a professor of philosophy who became a dean of the University of Prague in 1401. At the time the faculty of the university, like the hierarchy of the Church in Bohemia, was largely German. Hus was the leader of the Czech faction at the university, which was at issue with the Germans on a number of theological questions. He and his supporters were admirers of the works of John Wycliff, the English theologian who toward the end of the 14th Century had criticized the hierarchy of the Roman Church, still then the official Church of Britain. Wycliff had also supported the British Parliament in its refusal to pay tribute to Pope Urban V, and suggested that man could attain the grace of God and, therefore, enter into the kingdom of heaven without the aid or intercession of the clergy.

When Hus started to propagate Wycliff's views in Bohemia, the German faculty members, suspicious of national deviations, whether British or Czech, denounced the English theologian and ordered many of his works to be publicly burned. Hus insisted that Wycliff's views were being distorted and vigorously defended his position. Hus held the position of confessor to Queen Sophy, wife of Wenceslas IV, King of Bohemia, but even that could not protect him. He was excommunicated, and in 1415 the Holy Roman Emperor Sigismund, Wenceslas' brother, handed him over to the Church Council of Constance, where he was tried as a heretic and finally burned at the stake.

BRILLIANT ASTRONOMER, the Pole Nicholas Copernicus laid the foundation of modern astronomy in *De Revolutionibus Orbium Coelestium*, a work published in 1543 which set forth the theory that all the planets revolved around the sun.

Hus's execution aroused indignation throughout Bohemia, increased anti-German feeling and greatly strengthened the Hussite movement. There were public demonstrations against Sigismund. Successions to thrones, even by now, were not automatic and hereditary. King Wenceslas died in 1419. Sigismund was his heir, but the Czechs would have none of the Emperor for the Bohemian crown. On June 3, 1421, the Bohemian Diet, a parliament of nobles, declared Sigismund "unworthy" to sit on the Bohemian throne. The forces of the Emperor thereupon launched several crusades against the rebellious Hussites. The Czechs won a number of victories, but fell to quarreling among themselves. The Hussite movement divided into two principal factions—the

relatively moderate Utraquists, who advocated compromise and negotiation with Rome, and the radical Taborites. The split between them erupted into civil war. The Utraquists were eventually victorious, and after they had made an uneasy peace with Rome in 1434, Bohemia finally accepted Sigismund as its King in 1436.

The struggle had been pursued, however, with all the bitterness of religious fanaticism, and it had left Bohemia exhausted, embittered and disillusioned.

The Hussite movement, however, was by no means dead. Peter Chelčický, a scholar who condemned the use of force and rejected the authority of both the Catholic hierarchy and that of the state, founded an organization called the Bohemian Brethren. It was to become a powerful vehicle of Bohemian national aspirations, and the ideas promulgated by the Brethren prepared the ground for the Protestant Reformation which swept rapidly through Eastern Europe in the early part of the 16th Century. "We were all Hussites without being aware of it," said Martin Luther.

In 1526 the throne of Bohemia came to Archduke Ferdinand I of Austria, brother of the Habsburg Holy Roman Emperor Charles V. The accession of the Roman Catholic Habsburgs signaled the beginning of a bitter struggle between the Crown and the Protestant Bohemian Estates for supremacy in the political and religious government of the kingdom. The Habsburgs during the 16th Century made repeated attempts to suppress non-Catholic elements, particularly the Bohemian Brethren. Ferdinand I, who succeeded his brother as Emperor in 1556, called in the Jesuits to help reconvert the Bohemians to the Roman Church, but neither force nor Jesuitic argument met with success, and Lutheran influence continued to spread. During the reign of Rudolf II the Protestants finally managed to secure recognition. A "Letter of Majesty," signed by Rudolf on July 9, 1609, as a matter of political expediency, guaranteed them virtually complete religious freedom, as well as the right to elect *"defensores"* from among their number to see that the letter's provisions were carried out. Despite this agreement, however, friction continued. Meeting in the spring of 1618 to protest the closing of two of their churches, the members of the Bohemian Estates reached the conclusion that their only course was revolt. Led by Count Heinrich Matthias von Thurn, the nobles threw three Habsburg officials out of a window of Hradčany Castle in Prague, a form of political violence peculiar to the Czechs called defenestration (from the Latin *fenestra,* or "window").

THUS began a struggle which, lasting from 1618 to 1648, came to be known as the Thirty Years' War. As region after region rejected or declared its support of the Holy Roman Emperor, the conflict spread through most of Central and Northern Europe. In 1619 the Bohemian Estates refused to accept Rudolf's cousin Ferdinand II, soon to be elected Holy Roman Emperor, as King of Bohemia; instead they chose Frederick V of the Palatinate, one of the German nobles entitled to cast a ballot in the election of a Holy Roman Emperor. A Calvinist, Frederick was a leader of the Protestant faction within the Empire. The imperial Army met the Bohemians at a hill known as the White Mountain, on the outskirts of Prague, in November 1620. The forces of Emperor Ferdinand crushed Frederick's army; the rebel leaders were executed or exiled, and their lands were confiscated. Because of the brevity of his reign, Frederick became known as "the Winter King." Catholicism was declared Bohemia's sole faith, and German became an official language, together with Czech. Silent and apathetic, Bohemia suffered armies to cross and recross its territory. Towns were burned; the countryside was laid waste. The population in 1618 had been an estimated three million; it was but 900,000 in 1648, says the historian Henry F. Schwarz.

When we read about the ideological-dynastic struggles of these times, it seems to us that Eastern Europe could not possibly take any more bloodshed. But those were not the only wars that the people of the region had to endure. Aggressive new powers to the east had been rising since the 14th Century. After

the conquest of most of the Balkans the Moslem Ottoman Turks began to threaten Hungary in the early 15th Century. There had been little successful opposition to their expansion until János Hunyady, a professional soldier who had risen to command of the Hungarian army, drove the Turks from Transylvania and Serbia in 1434. He won additional acclaim by defeating the Moslem besiegers of Belgrade, in present-day Yugoslavia, in 1456. Hunyady's youngest son, Mátyás, was elected to the Hungarian throne in 1458. Mátyás created a standing army, built a chain of defenses around Hungary, reformed the constitution and equalized taxes. His legal reforms were of great benefit to the country, and his people dubbed him "the Just." He was also a patron of the arts and learning, and his collections of illuminated manuscripts and art objects were among the finest of his age.

Mátyás was able to impose a degree of control over the great landowners, called magnates in Hungary, but after his death in 1490 national unity collapsed. Suleiman the Magnificent, Sultan of Turkey, marched into Hungary with an army of 100,000 men and 300 cannons and overwhelmed the Hungarian army at the Battle of Mohács in 1526.

FOR more than a century and a half Hungary was a partitioned country: central Hungary was occupied by the Turks; Transylvania was governed by a succession of native rulers; Royal Hungary, the western fringe of the old kingdom, was ruled by the Habsburgs. In Turkish Hungary the government was absolute; native political life and culture were stifled; the land was distributed in fief to Turkish officials; and one fifth of all revenue was reserved for Allah. Peasants were slaughtered or sold into slavery in Turkey. Villages fell into dust, and fields reverted to swamp and brush.

Poland had similar troubles with its eastern neighbors in the same period. In addition to the constant thrust of Moslem expansion, threats were being felt to the vast Polish state from a new power known as Muscovy, centered around the strategically located city of Moscow on the central Russian plain. After the Jagiełłonian line died out in 1572, Stephen Batory, Duke of Transylvania, had come to the Polish throne. He proved to be a resolute military leader, three times defeating the armies of the Russian Czar, Ivan the Terrible. But on the death of Batory in 1586 Poland fell into the contemporary quarrels over religious and dynastic problems. The unity of the old Jagiełłonian empire began to crumble. The Ukrainian Cossacks had long resisted the efforts of Polish landowners in the Ukraine to reduce them to serfdom, and in 1648 they launched a major revolt. The diversion gave the ambitious Charles X Gustavus of Sweden the opportunity of invading Poland from the north. Shortly thereafter the Turks invaded from the southeast.

NOT inappropriately, the period is known in Polish history as "the deluge." The country was devastated. Gradually, however, the Poles rallied and, by skillful employment of the arts of diplomacy as well as arms, ejected the invaders from most of the Polish state, but not before they had lost half of their Ukrainian territory.

Two engagements in which the Poles were successful against the Turks had been won by Jan Sobieski, who emerged as the "savior of the country" and was elected King in 1674. In an effort to work out a system of Christian alliances which would strengthen Central and Eastern Europe against the Turks, Sobieski made a pact with Leopold I of Austria, the Holy Roman Emperor. But before Poland had need of Leopold, Austria needed Sobieski: the Turks, on a great drive toward Western Europe, arrived at the gates of Vienna in 1683. Enthusiastically supported by the Polish nation, Sobieski went to the rescue of Vienna and Christendom with an army of 30,000 men. There Sobieski combined forces with the army of Charles of Lorraine and drove back the Turks. By 1699 the Turks had been finally defeated, and thereafter they ceased to be an active threat to Eastern and Western Europe.

In this narrative the name Habsburg has been frequently mentioned; the moment has come to look more closely at the Habsburgs. The word is a condensation of *Habichtsburg,* the "hawk's castle" in Switzerland where the family had its origin in the 11th Century. Beginning as dukes and archdukes of Austria, the Habsburgs extended their influence throughout the European continent by contract-marriage alliances with other ruling families, to

such an extent that it was said, "Let others wage war; thou, happy Austria, marry." By 1522 the Habsburg Emperor Charles V controlled so much of Europe that he assigned the Austrian dominions to his brother Ferdinand I. In 1526, as a result of a typical Habsburg marriage alliance, Ferdinand became King of both Bohemia and Royal Hungary. Ferdinand and his son Maximilian subsequently established the basis of absolute Habsburg rule which was to last nearly 400 years.

Briefly ousted from their Hungarian possessions by the Turkish drive on Vienna in 1683, the Habsburgs treated the region as a conquered country when their armies returned after Sobieski's victory. This caused so much dissatisfaction that a group of Hungarian nobles opened secret negotiations with the retreating Turks. The conspiracy was exposed, and hundreds of Hungarian noblemen lost their lands and some their lives.

WHEN the Austrians took over all of Hungary after a final peace had been signed with the Turks, they found that the country had been devastated and virtually denuded of population. In an area of considerably more than 100,000 square miles, there were fewer than four million people; inhabited places were often a day's journey apart. But mindful of the disaffected Hungarian nobility and the number of Protestants, the Roman Catholic Austrians took no risks whatever; local estates were seized and sold, a new wave of German settlers moved into the old communal lands, the Protestants were persecuted. In 1687 the Hungarian constitution was amended to make the monarchic succession hereditary in the male line of the Habsburgs. Joseph I, son of Leopold I, the Habsburg incumbent, was thereupon crowned King of Hungary.

Reaction to the iron Habsburg rule took the form of a spontaneous popular rebellion led by Ferenc Rákóczi. After seven years of skirmishing, the rebellion ended in victory for the Habsburgs in 1711. Rákóczi and his entourage went into exile. His name would live long in Hungarian annals (the "Rákóczi March" by John Bihari is also the theme of Franz Liszt's *Hungarian Rhapsody No. 15*), but the fact was that Hungary, like Bohemia, was now firmly under the Habsburg heel.

In the hills near Gyöngyös, Hungary, a farm region of thatched roofs and clay walls, a woman carries a bucket through her village.

Agriculture: Major Asset and Major Problem

Poland, Czechoslovakia and Hungary lie at the heart of Europe's "agricultural half." Before the coming of Communism the three countries exported substantial amounts of grain. Nevertheless, production was held down by poor soil, primitive cultivation techniques and overcrowding in rural areas. The Communists, while strenuously pressing industrialization, have tried to raise efficiency by gathering private holdings into large, state-owned farms. These "collectives" have helped in some regions, failed in others. In general, despite radical reorganization, the countryside looks much as it did centuries ago.

COLLECTIVE FARMS are virtually as regulated as are large-scale industries

BEHIND UPENDED BICYCLES women harvest beets on a collective farm in Tura, Hungary. About 96 per cent of Hungary's farmland is socialized, as is 90 per cent of Czechoslovakia's. Poland, on the other hand, has de-emphasized collectivization in recent years, and 87 per cent of the land remains in private hands—although collectivization remains the official policy.

IN THE OFFICE of the Friendship Farm, a collective in Czechoslovakia, women stable hands consult with office workers. The farm employs 180 people; only men labor in the fields.

IN THE STABLES of the collective farm in Tura, Hungary, a foreman inspects dairy cows. Hungary lags considerably behind neighboring countries in the number of cattle it raises.

IN THE CANTEEN of the Tura collective *(below)* workers eat a lunch of soup and noodles, for which they pay a small sum. The average Hungarian farm worker makes about $14 a week.

STRANGELY ROUNDED HILLS rise behind three Polish Boy Scouts hitchhiking with a required "auto-stopper" sign in the Carpathian foothills near the Czech border. Despite their spectacular steepness, the hills have been cultivated for centuries.

POWER LINES and suspension cables carrying containers of coal *(left)* march across the rolling land of the Transdanubian region of Hungary, where a shepherd drives his flock homeward. The lines lead to the thriving mining town of Várpalota.

PRIVATE PLOT in eastern Hungary, on which corn and grapes are grown, is cultivated by a lone worker *(opposite)*. Only a small percentage of Hungary's land is given over to private holdings, but they grow a high proportion of the country's produce.

HARVESTING, *despite some mechanization, remains arduous work*

APPLE PICKERS on a collective farm at Tura, Hungary, reach the top of a tree from a ladder *(right)*. Large fruit crops—especially apples, plums and apricots—can be grown in Hungary because of the favorable climate: a high average temperature and cloudless summer days.

POTATO LOADERS wait for a truck *(opposite)* to haul away full sacks on a collective farm near Austerlitz, Czechoslovakia. Farm machinery is more plentiful in Czechoslovakia than in other Communist countries, but the quality is poor and spare parts are in short supply.

A TEAM OF WOMEN works in a potato field on the Austerlitz collective *(below)*. Farming has become a less attractive trade in recent years; many young men have left for industrial jobs, and some workers have resisted collectivization by conscious inefficiency and carelessness.

FINE HORSES *raised in the region remain important to the largely unmechanized agricultural economy*

STEPPING HIGH, a team of Lippizaners, a breed common in Hungary and nearby Austria, draws a coach on a farm in Hungary, where they are trained for international competition. Eastern Europe raises many horses, generally for less decorous work than that performed by these Lippizaners. In Poland horses are so numerous that they eat more grain than the nation's people.

KEEPING WATCH on horses *(left)* belonging to a collective farm, a rider gazes across the Hortobágy steppe. Stretching 186 miles west of Debrecen, the Hortobágy is the "Far West" of Hungary, a treeless plain where mirages are seen in the hot summers. Horsemen like this one, called *csikósok*, have for centuries worn these wide, pleated trousers and loose cloaks.

THE IMMEMORIAL LANDSCAPE is slowly altering as industry arrives

AN INDUSTRIAL HAZE rises behind a field near Nowa Huta, Poland, as a farmer guides his plow horses. The mills, part of the Lenin Steel Works built in 1949 to take advantage of the labor of a surplus rural population in need of employment, produce about three million tons of steel yearly. Burgeoning Nowa Huta now has a population of more than 100,000.

3

Crucible
of
Revolution

THE history of the 18th and 19th Centuries in Eastern Europe is the story of the struggle to preserve national identity. As parts of the Habsburg Empire, the old Kingdoms of Bohemia and Hungary were governed from Vienna, the imperial capital, and in both countries German came to be the language of the ruling classes. Whatever remained of the Bohemian and Hungarian national characters was preserved in the speech and customs of the peasants, artisans and shopkeepers. When nationalist movements revived in those countries, their leaders therefore concentrated their efforts on raising the native languages to official status. In Poland, on the other hand, the native language remained firmly

entrenched, and the problem of preserving national identity was territorial: with diminishing success the Poles struggled to maintain the integrity of their ethnic frontiers against incursions by Russia in the east and by Prussia and Austria in the west.

Polish independence had virtually ended with the death of Jan Sobieski in 1696. The kings who succeeded him were imposed on the country by foreign powers; Poland lost all control over its foreign policy. Efforts to carry out internal reforms were also effectively blocked by the country's neighbors, who had every interest in keeping Poland weak. Polish fortunes reached an ebb in 1697, when Russia and Prussia placed Frederick Augustus the Strong, the

Elector of Saxony, on the Polish throne. As Augustus II he proceeded to involve the country in a disastrous war with Sweden. At the war's end Poland was so weakened that its neighbors began openly discussing dividing the country among themselves.

The Poles reacted by choosing Stanislas Leszczyński, a patriotic Polish nobleman, for the throne when Augustus II died in 1733. Stanislas had the advantage of a dynastic connection with the reigning Bourbon family of France, but Austria and Russia feared French influence in Eastern Europe. Russia invaded the country, and at the end of a two-year conflict (which came to be known as the War of the Polish Succession), Stanislas was forced in 1735 to cede the throne to Augustus III, son of Augustus II.

THE new King proved totally disinterested in Poland and spent almost his entire reign in Dresden, leaving the affairs of state in the hands of a succession of court favorites. The political freedoms which Poland had achieved under the liberal Jagieł-łonian kings now proved a disadvantage. Any member of the Sejm, or parliament, could, under the right of the "free veto," dissolve the Sejm and thus annul its decisions. Foreign powers used the free veto to their own ends, bribing individual deputies to paralyze parliamentary action. Political reform was urged by Father Stanislas Konarski, a prominent educator, but with little success. In this state of indecision Russian armies were able to move at will across Poland, and to gain power and prestige in the affairs of Europe for a new Czarina, Catherine the Great.

On the death of Augustus III in 1763, however, Poland's powerful neighbors realized that it would be politically advantageous to place a native king on the Polish throne. Catherine and Prussia's Frederick the Great agreed to the crowning of Stanislas Augustus Poniatowski, former Polish Ambassador to Russia and one of Catherine's many lovers. Catherine favored him because she was convinced that he would never oppose her will, Frederick because he believed that Prussia might gain if a weak king were on the throne. Poniatowski was a nobleman of refinement and culture, and as King Stanislas Augustus he did much to revive the sagging intellectual life of Poland by fostering education and the arts. He could not, however, cope with powerful adversaries like

Catherine and Frederick, whose constant aim was to keep Poland in a state of anarchy. In 1768 Catherine overreached herself; a national insurrection broke out in protest against Russian interference in Polish affairs. The rebellion, led by members of the Pułaski family, had sporadic success, notably at the battle at Częstochowa, in which the Russian Army was routed. However, an unsuccessful attempt by the rebels to abduct Stanislas Augustus hastened the collapse of the movement and gave the great powers the excuse they were seeking to dismember Poland. It was obvious, they contended, that the country had fallen into chaos and anarchy.

In 1772, on the initiative of Prussia, the First Partition of Poland took place. Catherine annexed parts of the eastern provinces; Frederick took Polish Pomerania; the Empress Maria Theresa of Austria seized Galicia, in which lay Cracow and Lwów. Stanislas Augustus retained the Polish throne, but his kingdom had been reduced in area by one third.

The shock of the First Partition accelerated the internal reform movement which had been launched by Father Konarski and others. The educational system was overhauled, and the universities again became centers of intellectual life. Efforts were made to organize a national army of 100,000 men. In a new constitution promulgated in 1791 the Sejm abolished the troublesome free veto and curbed the power of the nobles. Most importantly the monarchy was made hereditary rather than elective.

ALL these developments were watched with suspicion by Russia, and in 1792, acting on an appeal from a group of disgruntled Polish nobles, the Russians invaded Poland. In 1793 Catherine annexed another large slice of the eastern provinces, and Frederick William II of Prussia took what remained of western Poland. A humiliated parliament was forced to acquiesce to this, the Second Partition of Poland. By it Poland was reduced to an 80,000-square-mile area, half the size it had been after the First Partition, and was occupied by Russian troops.

There were those, however, who refused to acquiesce. In a dramatic speech in the town square of Cracow in March 1794, Tadeusz Kościuszko, a member of an old Polish family who had been commissioned a major general in the Polish Army after

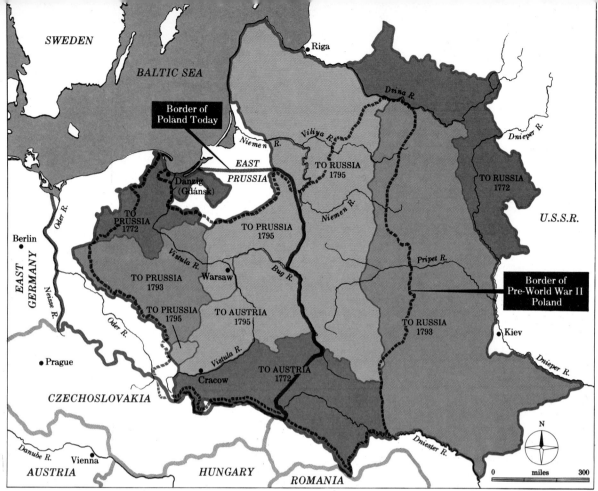

On the map, the following labels appear:

SWEDEN

BALTIC SEA

Riga

Dvina R.

Dnieper R.

Border of Poland Today

Niemen R.

Viliya R.

EAST PRUSSIA

TO RUSSIA 1795

TO RUSSIA 1772

Danzig (Gdánsk)

TO PRUSSIA 1772

TO PRUSSIA 1795

Niemen R.

U.S.S.R.

Berlin

Oder R.

EAST GERMANY

Neisse R.

TO PRUSSIA 1793

Vistula R.

Warsaw

Bug R.

Pripet R.

Border of Pre-World War II Poland

Oder R.

TO PRUSSIA 1795

TO AUSTRIA 1795

TO RUSSIA 1793

Kiev

Prague

Vistula R.

Cracow

TO AUSTRIA 1772

Dnieper R.

N

CZECHOSLOVAKIA

Dniester R.

Danube R.

Vienna

0   miles   300

AUSTRIA

HUNGARY

ROMANIA

THE PARTITIONS OF POLAND in the latter part of the 18th Century are illustrated on the map above. The country's land-hungry neighbors, Russia, Prussia and Austria, first seized Polish land in 1772. The next partition took place in 1793, when only Russia and Prussia took territory; and a final partition occurred in 1795, with all three strong neighbors again involved.

The last partition literally removed Poland, once a free country of some 280,000 square miles, from the face of the map. The areas that went to each neighbor in each partition are shown on the map in different shades of red, bounded by thin red lines. After World War I Poland was reconstituted as a nation *(dotted line)*. Its boundaries changed again after World War II.

rendering distinguished service to the rebel cause in the American Revolution, called upon the people to rise against the Russians. Supported by the peasants and remnants of the national army, Kościuszko defeated the Russians at the Battle of Racławice in April. Shortly afterward Warsaw and Wilno were liberated by his forces. The Polish troops were moving toward Prussian-held territory when the Prussians entered the war. They managed to join forces with the Russians, and the Poles were overwhelmed at the Battle of Maciejowice in October 1794.

The Third Partition of Poland followed in 1795. Russia took what was left of the eastern provinces; Prussia seized most of central Poland, including Warsaw; and Austria helped itself to what was left of the south. Western Europe, involved in the intricate international maneuvering which took place after the French Revolution of 1789, had no eyes for

the fate of a nation which, after 800 years of independence, had vanished from the map.

It was left to Napoleon to restore Poland. Because the partitioning powers, Russia, Austria and Prussia, were at war with France, many Polish volunteers joined the French forces. After Napoleon had defeated Russia, Austria and Prussia during the 1805-1807 campaigns, the territories lost to Prussia in the last two partitions were restored to Poland. The re-established state was named the Duchy of Warsaw. Two years later, when war between Austria and France broke out again, the Poles succeeded in liberating most of the territory seized by Austria during the Third Partition.

Then, in the summer of 1812, Napoleon launched a campaign against Russia. For a time it seemed successful; Napoleon's forces advanced deep into Russia. As a loyal supporter of Napoleon, Poland had good reason to believe that it would soon regain the eastern provinces lost to Russia under the partitions. Some 96,000 Poles threw themselves into the war against Russia. But the Russians fell back, refusing to give battle and burning the earth behind them. Overextended, without supplies as the Russian winter set in, Napoleon's troops were forced to retreat westward after briefly occupying Moscow. On their heels came a Russian army which occupied the Duchy of Warsaw.

At the Congress of Vienna, which followed Napoleon's final defeat in 1815, Czar Alexander I demanded hegemony over Poland, but the conference powers, afraid of giving Russia too much, decided to partition Poland once more. Part of the Duchy of Warsaw, including Poznań and Toruń, was returned to Prussia. Cracow was made into a tiny republic. What remained was declared to be the Kingdom of Poland—a kingdom in permanent union with Russia, whose king was to be the Russian Czar.

All such arrangements, however, failed to take into account the capacity of the Poles for battle in the face of overwhelming odds. In November 1830 the youth of Warsaw revolted against Russian domination. A revolutionary national government was set up under the leadership of Prince Adam Czartoryski, a prominent Polish diplomat, and a formal war developed between Poland and Russia. The Polish Army fought bravely for nine months but was forced to retreat to Warsaw. After a siege of three weeks the city .fell to the Russians in September 1831. Condemned to death, Czartoryski fled to Britain and then to Paris, where he was followed by a steady stream of Polish political refugees.

Presently the Hôtel Lambert, Czartoryski's home in Paris, became an unofficial headquarters for the more conservative exiles. More radical, democratic refugees gathered around their old leader, Joachim Lelewel, former professor of history at the University of Wilno who had been dismissed by the Russian governor for spreading "unreasonable Polish nationalism by means of learning." Lelewel was an outspoken advocate of national insurrections; the French Government thought him dangerous and banished him. Lelewel moved to Brussels, where he wrote several important books on Polish history.

Among the visitors to the Hôtel Lambert was Adam Mickiewicz, who had been one of Lelewel's students at Wilno. After becoming a teacher he was arrested by the Russians for nationalist agitation and deported to Russia. During his four years in exile he composed his *Crimean Sonnets*, which established him as a great poet. In Paris after his release he wrote a masterpiece of Polish literature, a nostalgic epic entitled *Pan Tadeusz*, and was given the Chair of Slavonic Literature at the Collège de France. Also among the exiles was Juliusz Słowacki, a proud, aloof young man who had given the 1830-1831 insurrection two memorable songs, "Hymn to the Virgin" and "Song of the Rutheno-Lithuanian Legion." In exile Słowacki turned to drama and poetry. He exemplified the romanticism which then pervaded the Polish patriotic movement.

FOR the foreigner untuned to the cadences of the Polish language, the man who best conveys the spirit of Polish life at that time is Frédéric Chopin. Born in 1810, he became a musical prodigy who earned his living as a concert pianist. Chopin composed mazurkas and polonaises based on national dances and on the folk music which he absorbed while vacationing at the manor house of his friend Dominik Dziewanowski at the village of Zelazowa Wola near Warsaw. He was in Stuttgart in 1831

POLES WHO FOUGHT FOR AMERICA

Many Poles who fought against the oppressors of their nation in the late 18th Century were inspired by the American Revolution. Among them was Tadeusz Kościuszko, who came to America in 1777 after training in military academies in Warsaw and Paris. He organized the defenses of West Point, fought in the Saratoga campaign and returned to Poland with a sword inscribed by George Washington. Kazimierz Pułaski, a young Polish nobleman, joined the revolutionary army as a volunteer and rose to command his own cavalry unit. He was mortally wounded in the Battle of Savannah.

KAZIMIERZ PULASKI

TADEUSZ KOSCIUSZKO

when the news of the suppression of the Polish insurrection reached him. His anguish may be judged by a work he wrote immediately afterward: the *Etude in C Minor,* also known as *The Revolutionary,* a composition permeated with patriotic feeling.

THE fever of nationalism was not confined to the Poles; the other suppressed peoples of Eastern Europe became as deeply infected with it. The tenuous national identity which had been preserved in the folklore and language of the Czechs, Slovenes and Hungarians had been revived during the wave of romanticism which swept through the intellectual life of Europe at the beginning of the 19th Century. Scholars began to give the native languages serious attention. In Bohemia the Czech language, codified by the philologist Josef Dobrovský, provided a tool for vigorous native expression. A dictionary of the language compiled by Josef Jungmann and a history of the Czech people by František Palacký were illuminating works; gradually the people of Bohemia rediscovered the achievements of their ancestors and came to feel a kinship with other Slav nations. A parallel development occurred in Slovakia, where writers like Jan Kollár and Pavel Safařík recounted tales of Slav achievements.

In Hungary the Magyar tongue was spoken only by the peasants; the upper classes, as we have noted, spoke German, and the official language was Latin. However, a dilettante use of Magyar had kept the language sufficiently alive to make it a vehicle for the romantic poets. After the French Revolution some Magyar poets had been jailed. The arrests, however, succeeded only in creating wider interest in the Magyar language. In the Hungarian Diet in 1825 Count István Széchenyi declared that the "soul of a people resided in its language." He caused a sensation by donating a year's income for the study and improvement of Magyar. Széchenyi followed up his speech with attacks on the feudal constitution and taxation system of Hungary.

Széchenyi's ideas were taken up by the country's youth, who were led by Lajos Kossuth, a wellborn but impecunious lawyer. Given the editorship of a newspaper, Kossuth proved a brilliant exponent of the cause of Magyar nationalism and of social and economic reform. By 1843 the nationalist movement had become so strong that Prince Metternich, Foreign Affairs Minister of the Habsburg Empire, gave way to a demand that Magyar become the official language of government in Hungary. The protests of the non-Magyar minorities—the Serbs, Slovaks, Romanians and Croats—were overruled.

Hungary was riding a wave of nationalism, and there were calls for economic and social reforms as well. In need of Hungarian money and recruits for the imperial Army, Metternich realized that further concessions had to be made. In 1846 he appointed Count György Apponyi to the post of Chancellor of Hungary. Apponyi was the leader of a group of conservatives loyal to Vienna who nevertheless advocated some moderate reforms. Part of Apponyi's program was put into effect, but before the Diet met in 1847 Ferenc Deák, a leader of the reform movement, issued an "Oppositional Declaration." The document made no direct attack on the Habsburg Government, but it denounced Apponyi's regime as "foreign and nonnational." In addition, it called for such reforms as a Hungarian national ministry responsible to the Diet, taxation of the clergy and aristocracy, and extension of the franchise.

THE calls for liberty and for an end to autocracy were not, of course, confined to Hungary; they echoed across the European continent. The Hungarian Diet was in fact still in session in February 1848 when Paris revolted against the Bourbons, who had been reinstalled on the throne after Napoleon's downfall, and forced the abdication of King Louis Philippe. It was a turning point in time; from France revolution spread throughout Europe. Riots broke out in Prague; the people of Berlin and other German cities built barricades in the streets and called for constitutional government; in Vienna thousands of the subjects of the Emperor Ferdinand poured into their own streets with similar demands. Metternich fled and a revolutionary committee took over the imperial Government. The committee did not, however, depose the Emperor, a mistake which was to prove major. Throughout the year he used Habsburg monies and the brains of his supporters to recoup the imperial losses.

Events now moved at a bewildering pace. German liberals proposed that a new, federalized Germanic

Crucible of Revolution

state be established, which would include the multi-national Habsburg Empire. František Palacký, who emerged as the spokesman for the Czechs, protested that Bohemia could never become a part of a German state. Similar views were voiced at a Pan-Slav congress which opened in Prague in the spring of 1848. The Czechs repudiated the authority of the Vienna committee and established their own Government, insisting that they wanted autonomy, but autonomy within the Austrian, not a German, system. In June, riots erupted again in Prague; the Austrian Army, still loyal to the Emperor, marched into the city and dispersed the Slav congress.

WHEN the news of the 1848 revolution in Paris reached Hungary, Kossuth issued a declaration insisting on the need for responsible government, which was accepted by the Emperor Ferdinand, fearful of the loss of Hungary. A provisional ministry was thereupon formed under Count Lajos Batthyány, a liberal magnate. The ministry drew up a program similar to that of Déak's "Oppositional Declaration" of 1847, which the Diet proceeded to formulate. It called for limited monarchy, a Cabinet responsible to a bicameral parliament, universal taxation and religious freedom. The Emperor gave his approval to "the April laws," as the reforms were called, after the sensational month in which he accepted them, and to mass demonstrations of joy Batthyány was confirmed in office as head of the new ministry. But not everyone was satisfied; fearful of Magyar overlordship, the Romanian, Serb and Croatian minorities also demanded national rights.

The Austrian monarchists now saw their opportunity to utilize the national rivalries among the peoples of the region. They persuaded Colonel Josip Jellačić, the Habsburg viceroy of Croatia, to lead his army into southern Hungary. As the Croatian forces approached, Batthyány resigned and authority passed to Kossuth. As head of a newly established Committee of National Defense, he organized a volunteer army.

The last hope of compromise between the Habsburgs and the Hungarians vanished when the royal Plenipotentiary was lynched by a mob in Pest. The new Hungarian army then drove Jellačić and his Croatian forces back across the frontier. But the respite was only momentary; after quelling a renewed uprising in Vienna, Austrian military forces turned toward Hungary. On December 2, 1848, Ferdinand was persuaded to abdicate in favor of his young nephew Franz Josef, a move Kossuth interpreted as an attempt to free the monarchists from Ferdinand's promise to uphold the April laws. Kossuth declared the abdication illegal as far as Hungary was concerned, but in January the Austrians reached Budapest. Kossuth and his supporters fled, and an imperial manifesto issued the following March stated that Franz Josef ruled an "indissoluble constitutional Austrian Empire." But Kossuth was not yet defeated; the Hungarian army, under the brilliant leadership of Arthur Görgey, inflicted a series of defeats on the Austrians, and Kossuth proclaimed Hungary a fully independent and sovereign state. In Transylvania a long and resourceful campaign was carried on by Josef Bem, a Polish general, and Polish volunteers who had enlisted in the Hungarian cause to fight the oppressors of their own partitioned country.

The end, however, was in sight. Kossuth's declaration of independence and the military successes of the Hungarians prompted the Austrians to appeal to Czar Nicholas I of Russia for help. Fearing that the revolution might spread to his Polish dominions, Nicholas gladly obliged. In the summer of 1849 a Russian army moved in, and the Hungarians, outnumbered more than 3 to 1, were forced to surrender at the Battle of Világos. Kossuth and Bem fled to Turkey, while the remnants of the Hungarian army surrendered to the Russian marshal, Prince Ivan Paskievicz. He reported to the Czar: "Hungary lies vanquished at the feet of Your Majesty."

A REIGN of terror followed. Batthyány was executed, as were more than 100 other rebels. The Hungarians lost all the constitutional liberties they had won, and the country was placed under a military administration headed by the notoriously cruel General Julius von Haynau, who boasted in a proclamation that he "would see to it that there should be no more revolutions in Hungary for a hundred years."

Even before all resistance had been entirely quelled in Hungary, Emperor Franz Josef had dissolved the constituent assembly which had been convened in July 1848 to fashion a democratic constitution for the empire. For the next decade he ruled as an autocrat, centralizing the administration of the empire in Vienna. But autocracy was dying nonetheless; the battles of 1848 had not been fought entirely in vain. After the Austrian Army had suffered two serious defeats, one at the hands of the French in 1859 and another at the hands of the Prussians in 1866, Franz Josef was forced to amend his policies. In 1867, after years of negotiation and effort by Ferenc Deák, one of Hungary's greatest statesmen, Austria and Hungary signed an agreement which brought the Austro-Hungarian monarchy into being. Under the arrangement the two countries, linked by the Habsburg monarchy, were to function internally as autonomous units, although foreign, financial and defense matters were to be handled jointly. A similar arrangement was about to be reached with Bohemia, but protests by the Germans in Austria and Bohemia, as well as by the Hungarians, jealous of their new position, stayed the Emperor's hand. Until World War I Bohemia's political influence in Vienna was to be negligible.

DURING and after the 1848 revolutions Russia had intensified police repression in the Polish territories. The Polish exiles in Paris pinned their hopes on the French ruler, Napoleon III. When he declared war on Russia in 1854 and, with the British and the Turks, attacked the Crimea, a new future seemed to be dawning for Poland. But at the peace conference held in Paris in 1856 after the Russians had lost the war, the Poles failed to persuade Napoleon III to raise the Polish question.

Nevertheless, the setback produced by the Crimean defeat caused Czar Alexander II, successor to Nicholas I, to embark on a series of progressive reforms in Russia, and these changes made the more moderate Poles adopt a conciliatory policy toward the Russians. Their program found a determined spokesman in Marquis Alexander Wielopolski, who gradually won many liberal concessions from the Czar in the fields of education, language and economic development.

The idea of compromise with Russia failed, however, to win support from the radical Polish youth.

In 1863 Wielopolski instituted a military draft designed to disperse and silence his troublesome critics; instead it caused a general insurrection which spread beyond the borders of Poland into the partitioned regions. Sharp guerrilla actions were fought against the Russians by detachments of Poles who deserted from service in the Russian Army. The rebel leaders looked to France and England for help, but a series of halfhearted diplomatic moves had no effect on the Russians, who, by the summer of 1864, succeeded in suppressing the revolt. Poland was completely incorporated into the Russian Empire under the name Vistula Land, and the Polish question was declared a "domestic" issue by the Russians.

SO ended the 19th Century revolts against monarchic absolutism in Eastern Europe. Most historians agree that the major positive result was the freeing of serfs, which took place in all the countries, including Russia. A dispassionate observer of the events was Karl Marx, whose *Communist Manifesto*, published on the eve of 1848, had summoned the proletarians of all lands to unite in the fight against the bourgeois masters of the world. On the basis of Marx's exhortations a new generation of revolutionaries was to devise a technique of class struggle which would have a lasting impact on Eastern Europe.

In the meantime the region was carried along in the evolutionary process of industrial and scientific development. Railroads, steamships, coal and gas, telegraphs, newspapers and popular education were creating inside Eastern Europe an atmosphere in which the policies of German, Austrian and Russian absolutism could not long survive. The sense of nationhood was sustained by writers, artists and musicians. By the 1880s Czech had become the official language in many schools and regions of Bohemia, and was being employed in official documents. At the University of Prague nationalist agitation finally led to the separation of the Czech and German language groups into separate faculties.

Nationalism also found expression in the work of the musicians of the region. Of these, one of the most noted was Bedřich Smetana. Born in 1824, Smetana became a child prodigy. At the age of 30 he found the Germanized atmosphere of Prague so stifling that he went to Sweden, where he composed such orchestral works as *Richard III*, *Wallenstein's Camp* and *Haakon Jarl*. After returning to Prague in 1861 he wrote several patriotic operas and symphonic poems. His orchestral compositions glow with native color, and his Slav lyricism sets him apart from the great German composers of his day.

Antonín Dvořák was the son of a village innkeeper and at an early age played the violin at local festivities. After receiving lessons from a village organist he entered an organ school in Prague and played in orchestras for a dozen years. He had written two symphonies, chamber music, an opera and a host of songs when he was granted a Government stipend in 1875. Thereafter he became one of the most prolific composers in Europe, turning out oratorios, Masses and other works. Dvořák did not have to acquire a political attitude; by birth and native genius he was irreducibly Bohemian. Even his *New World Symphony*, despite its American themes, expresses romantic nostalgia for a small country.

Franz Liszt's father was a clerk employed on the Esterhazy estates in Hungary; his mother was Austrian. After hearing Paganini play the violin in Paris in 1831 he was inspired to perfect his own pianoforte technique. He became the greatest pianist of his time. Kind and generous, Liszt was the darling of the great salons and was given a patent of nobility in Vienna by the Emperor and presented with a Sword of Honor by the Hungarian magnates. Above all he is remembered for his Hungarian rhapsodies—spirited, intensely romantic music in the grand style. By the time of his death in 1886 his works had given Hungary immense cultural standing.

IN Poland not even the painters could keep politics out of their work. After the failure of the 1863 insurrection Jan Matejko, a Cracow artist, painted scores of historical pictures that profoundly affected the 19th and early-20th Century patriots. Although Matejko's canvases are vast and crowded, they manage to have an intensely personal flavor. Matejko became a professor of the School of Fine Arts and won gold medals and world acclaim, but he cared only to remind Poles of their glorious past.

A different kind of painter was Josef Chełmoński. Born in 1850, Chełmoński studied abroad for some years, then suddenly abandoned his studies and returned to Poland full of nostalgia for the landscapes of his youth. Considered Poland's finest realist, he delighted in painting scenes from rural life—galloping horses and peasants in the fields.

Popular education brought a huge new readership to the Polish author Henryk Sienkiewicz, who wrote several captivating novels on the historical past of his people. His most famous work is *Quo Vadis*, which deals with the persecution of the Christians under the Roman Emperor Nero. Another Polish novelist who achieved worldwide fame was Josef Konrad Korzeniowski. Young Korzeniowski went to sea in French and British sailing ships and, under the name Joseph Conrad, became a writer of novels in English, among them the minor classic, *Lord Jim*. "It does not seem to me," Conrad wrote, "that I have been unfaithful to my country by having proved to the English that a gentleman from the Ukraine can be as good a sailor as they, and has something to tell them in their own language." Two of his finer novels, *The Secret Agent* and *Under Western Eyes*, are about clandestine Russian political activity, already a European problem.

The Polish musical tradition also remained strong. Toward the end of the 19th Century a school of young musicians in Warsaw, inspired by the example of Chopin, also began using Polish folk-song themes in serious music. The most famous of these young musicians was Ignace Jan Paderewski. Although a highly original composer, he made his reputation as a virtuoso pianist. A critic who heard him play at Carnegie Hall in New York City in 1891 wrote that his playing could not be described; it had to be experienced. Inspired by the 40th anniversary of the 1863 insurrection, Paderewski wrote the *B Minor Symphony*, one of his finest works. In the world-shaking events of the 20th Century he was to be the most influential Pole of his day.

BY the opening of that century Eastern Europe had undergone many changes. Between 1848 and 1914 an estimated five million people immigrated to the United States from Eastern Europe, bringing with them a profound sense of the injustices of the old European regimes. At the same time a stream of Jewish refugees from the recurrent pogroms in Russia had been moving westward to swell the urban populations of the fast-growing cities. A powerful new German nation, fashioned out of the old Germanic principalities by the "Iron Chancellor," Otto von Bismarck, had risen in Europe. Bismarck was as hostile to Polish aspirations as was the Czar. Both therefore attempted to check any nationalist movements by instigating a policy of systematic oppression. The teaching of Polish was forbidden. Strikes were ruthlessly put down.

IN this atmosphere the Polish political parties which had come into being during the last decade of the 19th Century were forced to go underground. There were three parties on the Left and one important party on the Right. All were destined to play major roles in the coming history of Eastern Europe. Two of these parties were Marxist in character. One was the Social Democratic Party of Poland and Lithuania, led by Rosa Luxemburg. It insisted on cooperation with the Russian Social Democratic Party, led by Vladimir Lenin. The other Marxist party was the Bund, an exclusively Jewish group which differed with the Social Democrats only in that it demanded cultural autonomy for national minorities, especially for the Jews scattered throughout the czarist empire. The most important Leftist party at this stage, however, was the Polish Socialist Party. Under the leadership of Józef Piłsudski, a young patriot who had spent five years in Siberia, it became a paramilitary group for organized revolution. On the Right was the National Democratic Party. Under the leadership of Roman Dmowski, it favored a moderate and conservative policy of conciliation with the czarist Government.

After the defeat of Russia by the Japanese in the war of 1904-1905 and the abortive Russian Socialist revolt of 1905, the Czar issued promises that the Russian Empire (which included Poland) would be given a bill of rights and that elections would be held for a parliament. The Polish Socialist parties boycotted the election held in 1906, and Dmowski's National Democratic Party won all 36 Polish seats in the new Russian Duma, or parliament. A promise of autonomy for Poland did not materialize, however, although Russian administration became more relaxed. At about the same time Rosa Luxemburg's Social Democratic Party in effect merged with the Russian Social Democratic Party. Piłsudski thereupon moved away from the Socialists and in 1908 formed an organization called the Union of Active Resistance to fight Russian rule. In 1912 he began training an underground army.

In Bohemia the Young Czech Party emerged as the dominant political group. National consciousness had been fostered by the Sokol movement, an organization of gymnastic societies which promoted mass folk dances and the singing of patriotic songs. Another continuing center of nationalistic activity was the University of Prague, where Thomas Garrigue Masaryk held the Czech chair of philosophy. Masaryk had served several years in the ineffectual Vienna parliament, then formed his own Progressive Party in Bohemia in 1900. With Karel Kramář, leader of the Young Czechs, Eduard Beneš, a young university lecturer in Prague, and other political leaders, Masaryk organized a secret group which was committed to the idea of achieving complete independence for the Czech and Slovak peoples.

THERE was similar political ferment in Hungary, where the Government remained under the control of the conservative magnates. But the magnates themselves were discontented with Vienna's control of the joint Austro-Hungarian armies. Among the non-Magyar minorities unrest under Magyar rule was growing.

This was the situation in Eastern Europe at the beginning of the second decade of this century when an event occurred which put all the conflicting forces into violent play. The Slav states of the neighboring Balkans had for years been in an unsettled state, subject to the recurrent pressures and divergent ambitions of Russia, Prussia and Austria.

In 1908 the Habsburgs formally annexed the Serbian provinces of Bosnia and Hercegovina in present-day Yugoslavia. Attending military maneuvers in the annexed region some six years later, the Austrian Archduke Franz Ferdinand, heir presumptive to the aging Emperor Franz Josef, was assassinated by a Serb patriot. The date was June 28, 1914. There was a hushed pause while numerous alliances were called into effect, and less than two months later Europe was plunged into World War I.

NOVICE FLUTIST leads her singing classmates at Budapest's Szuzanna Lorantffy School. Most Hungarian primary schoolchildren are taught to sing and to play at least one instrument.

The Arts: Power, Grace and Dedication

Art has for centuries lived at the forefront of the national consciousness in Poland, Czechoslovakia and Hungary. Ever since Polish kings brought Renaissance painters and poets to their castles, high culture has found a favorable climate in Eastern Europe. A powerful instinct for music has produced such masters as Frédéric Chopin and Franz Liszt. Czechoslovakian theater and Polish films have long rivaled the world's best. Today the plastic arts are filled with vitality. For a time the Soviet insistence upon "socialist realism" in art—the photolike representation of heroic generals and bright-faced workers—seemed to bode ill for Eastern European culture. Nonetheless, artists and audiences alike have not allowed their heritage to be abridged.

POISED ORCHESTRA and chorus (*left*) await their conductor's signal at the distinguished Franz Liszt Academy of Music in Budapest. Concerts are almost always sold out in Hungary.

YOUNG VIOLINIST follows the direction of his instructor at Hungary's prestigious National Academy of Music. Founded in 1875 by the composer and pianist Franz Liszt, the academy has numbered among its students such 20th Century musicians as Béla Bartók and Zoltán Kodály. Both of them later joined its faculty. The academy now has more than 350 pupils.

RISING STAR of the Budapest Opera,
a young and gifted soprano performs
in a great musical tradition

PRACTICING AT HOME with her father, an accomplished pianist, Margit Laszlo works on a score. Still in her thirties, she is regarded as one of Hungary's finest young singers.

REHEARSING AN ARIA from an opera in her apartment *(below)*, Mrs. Laszlo entertains her husband and young son. She has been a member of the Budapest Opera company since 1953.

BEFORE A PERFORMANCE at the opera, an attendant gives a final touch to Mrs. Laszlo's hair. She performs at opera houses throughout Hungary and frequently makes foreign tours.

AFTER THE OPERA, Mrs. Laszlo sips coffee with her husband and friends at the Opera House Club. She receives about $375 a month from the opera, a high income in Hungary.

SINGING THE LEAD in the comic opera *L'Elisir d'Amore (below)*, Mrs. Laszlo plays a country girl. Trained at the Hungarian National Academy, she gives 60 performances a year.

TALENTED ARTISTS explore
new ideas and promising techniques
in a wide range of fields

POSTER MAKER, Waldemar Swierzy lights a cigarette in his Warsaw studio. Posters, which have evolved into a highly creative art form, are widely used for advertising in Europe.

CZECH PUPPETEER, Jiří Trnka demonstrates the painstaking technique of producing movies with puppet actors. The position of each puppet is minutely altered as each frame is shot.

PROMINENT PAINTER, István Kurucz entertains friends beneath the simple peasant pitchers and plates he collects in his Budapest studio. His paintings often employ peasant themes.

AVANT-GARDE SCULPTOR, Marian Kruczek is surrounded by samples of his work in his studio at Nowa Huta, Poland. He constructs insectlike sculptures from steel scrap and plaster.

COMMERCIAL ILLUSTRATOR, Victor Gorka, a Pole, stands before some of his recent posters *(left)*. Unlike popular commercial art, "pure" painting in Poland is generally abstract.

COMPOSER'S HOUSE in a village outside Warsaw receives a constant stream of visitors curious to see where Frédéric Chopin was born in 1810. Poles generally consider Chopin the most towering cultural figure their country has produced.

MAGNIFICENT TAPESTRY shows two satyrs displaying a royal crest of Poland *(opposite)*. This masterpiece, which once decorated the tent of a 16th Century Polish king, is housed, together with other art treasures, in Wawel Castle in Cracow.

RENAISSANCE PAINTINGS of the 15th Century are examined by schoolchildren in the hall of a fortress in Marienburg, Poland. Built near Danzig in the 13th Century by the Teutonic Knights, Marienburg was once a mighty European stronghold.

EXQUISITE ARTICLES from
a martial era are preserved
at Wawel Castle in Cracow, Poland

TROPHY OF WAR, this jewel-studded shield was captured at the Battle of Vienna in 1683, in which Polish legions under Jan Sobieski defeated Turkish armies.

PAPAL GIFT, a velvet hat *(below)* bears the dove symbol of the Holy Ghost embroidered in pearls. The Pope presented it to Sobieski after the Battle of Vienna.

GOLDEN HILTS of 16th Century swords suggest the opulence loved by Poland's aristocratic warriors. The sword at the left has two pistols set along the blade.

DAZZLING RAIMENT, this gold-embroidered robe *(opposite)* was presented to Jan Sobieski by the French King Louis XIV in honor of the crucial Vienna victory.

Rise
and Fall
of Nations

WORLD WAR I, that great continental divide of history, was drawing to a close, and to the leaders of the Central Powers it was apparent that they would not emerge the victors. Seeking to salvage what he could, Charles, the new Habsburg Emperor of Austria-Hungary, had sent out peace feelers, offering autonomy to the Czechs, Slovaks and Hungarians within a federalized Habsburg state. But the tides of nationalism were at the flood; after centuries of bitterness and oppression and the immediate ravages of the war, the peoples of Eastern Europe were of no mood to accept the last olive branch of the last Habsburg Emperor. Already committed to a policy of self-determination for Eastern

Europe, in considerable measure because of the dedicated urgings of President Woodrow Wilson of the United States, the Allied powers rejected Charles's offer and launched an offensive from the Balkans which had as its objective the final destruction of the old Austro-Hungarian Empire. In October 1918, only a month before the Armistice which brought the war to a close, the Czech nationalist leader Thomas Masaryk, who had fled Prague on the outbreak of the war and had gone to the United States, issued a declaration proclaiming the independence of a new nation to be called Czechoslovakia. In Paris the Czecho-Slovak National Council, which Masaryk and his fellow patriot Eduard Beneš had set up to agitate for independence, was recognized by the Allies as the provisional government of the country.

Within days the war was over. In Prague an undercover National Committee emerged into the open and took over the government from the defeated Austrians. Masaryk was elected President of Czechoslovakia; Karel Kramář, leader of the Young Czech Party, was named Premier; Beneš became Foreign Minister. Czechoslovakia was in existence—but it was an odd admixture. The new country was a conjunction of Bohemia and Moravia, which had been part of the old Habsburg Empire, and Slovakia and Ruthenia, which had both been for many years a part of Hungary.

In Poland events had moved equally swiftly. There, on the outbreak of the war, Józef Piłsudski, the founder of the Polish League of Active Resistance, had allied himself with the Austrians against czarist Russia. Like other Eastern European nationalist leaders, he hoped to use the struggle between his country's longtime oppressors to advance the cause of independence. His irregulars, armed by the Austrians and soon reinforced to the strength of an army corps, attacked the Russians and fought a series of gallant engagements before being forced to retreat.

DURING the summer of 1915, however, an Austro-German offensive pushed the Russians back beyond the borders of Poland. The Kingdom of Poland was nominally restored by the Central Powers in an effort to win Polish support for their cause, and Piłsudski took a seat on the Council of State set up by the conquerors. But he was soon disillusioned. The Germans began dismantling Polish factories and removing machinery to Germany, together with thousands of Polish forced laborers. When Piłsudski refused to integrate his legions into the German Army he was arrested by the Germans and jailed. Meanwhile, Roman Dmowski, Piłsudski's political rival and leader of the National Democratic Party, had left Poland for Paris. There he persuaded the French Government to authorize the formation in France of a Polish army of expatriates and refugees to fight the Germans. With Ignace Paderewski, the celebrated Polish concert pianist, Dmowski also set up a Polish National Committee. Together the two men began a campaign for Polish independence.

Ironically, the Germans were to bring the Poles' dreams of independence to fruition. On November 10, 1918, one day before the Armistice, the Germans released Piłsudski from prison and sent him by special train to Warsaw.

PILSUDSKI was a man to be reckoned with. Born in one of the eastern provinces of Poland which had been so often occupied by the Russians, he was an uncompromising Polish patriot. A passage from his memoirs describes his feelings as a youth in Russian prison camps: "Helpless fury and shame that I could do nothing to hinder my enemies often stifled me; my cheeks burned that I must suffer in silence while my pride was trampled upon, listening to lies and scornful words about Poland, Poles and their history." In the confusions and miseries of postwar Europe he saw only one goal: a strong Poland.

In Warsaw Piłsudski began assembling a national defense force with the remnants of the legions he had successfully led against the Russians in the first year of the war. His prestige was high, and the Polish National Committee in Paris, with which the Allies had been dealing, sent Paderewski to Warsaw to talk to him. The two men agreed that a constitutional government should be established. A general election was held in January 1919, and sovereignty was invested in a newly formed parliament in which the leaders of the Paris National Committee took leading positions. Paderewski, as Prime Minister and Foreign Minister, and Dmowski then attended the Versailles Peace Conference, where they brilliantly presented the case for a democratic Poland. The real power, however, still lay in the hands of Piłsudski, whom parliament elected chief of state.

Hungary, too, was caught up in the swirl of events. The Hungarians had gone to war reluctantly, but had fought loyally beside the Austrians to protect their position in the Austro-Hungarian Empire. Two weeks before the Armistice Count Mihály Károlyi, a magnate who had been agitating for Hungarian independence, set up a National Council in Budapest to demonstrate his opposition to the old empire. Emperor Charles appointed him Minister-President, and in this capacity Károlyi opened negotiations with the Allies for a separate peace. It was too late; the move failed to prevent the Allied armies from occupying all but the western provinces of Hungary. Charles renounced further participation in the peace negotiations, and on November 16, 1918, the National Council dissolved parliament and proclaimed a republic. Károlyi became President, but when the Allied powers, determined to treat Hungary as a defeated belligerent, occupied still more territory, he resigned.

So the war was over, and political independence for much of Eastern Europe was at last a reality. Yet independence was no panacea for Eastern Europe. Trying to draw reasonable territorial frontiers in a region where races, religions and languages overlapped in every direction was virtually impossible. After the Peace Conference had adjourned it was found that more than 30 per cent of the people of the new Czechoslovak republic were neither Czechs nor Slovaks nor Ruthenians. For the most part they were Germans who had moved in with the Habsburgs.

Understandably, none of the new regimes was satisfied. Poland's access to the sea had been reduced to a narrow corridor, and Danzig, its major port on the Baltic, had been made a "free city" under League of Nations control. To guard against efforts by its German peoples to attach themselves to neighboring Austria, Czechoslovakia garrisoned the Austrian frontier. It also fought a short battle with Poland over the border province of Teschen. The Slovaks complained that the Czechs had failed to honor a promise of Slovak autonomy made at the inception of Czechoslovakia. Hungary had lost 70 per cent of its prewar territories to enlarged or newly created neighbors, and some three million ethnic Magyars were now outside its borders.

The victorious Allied powers might have paid closer attention to the problems of territories and minorities had they been less concerned about the intentions of Bolshevik Russia. Their apprehensions

were understandable. Postwar conditions were chaotic. In Poland 12 per cent of the country's villages had been destroyed; factories were in ruins; and the transport system was almost nonexistent. Unemployment, profiteering, near-famine conditions and epidemics of typhoid were everywhere in Eastern Europe. Many men returning from the eastern fronts brought with them an aroma of Bolshevism. Communist movements appeared in Austria, Hungary and Poland. In Germany a revolution was launched by the Communists. They failed to win power, but the victory over them was to prove costly. Russian participation in such revolutions—ostensibly in the interests of the international proletariat, but actually, as it turned out, for the furtherance of the goals of the Russian state—had the effect of provoking violent nationalist reactions among the middle classes of the disturbed countries. Soon counterrevolutionary and national revolutionary organizations of various types began to appear, one of which was the German National Socialist (Nazi) Party.

Among the many revolutionaries who entered the lists at this time was Béla Kun, a former Hungarian prisoner of war in Russia who had taken a part in the Bolshevik Revolution. Immediately after the war Kun arrived in Budapest, where he organized a Hungarian Communist Party. Gaining the support of the Social Democratic Party, he took over the Government in March 1919. Kun emulated the Bolsheviks by nationalizing all larger enterprises and by announcing plans for the collectivization of the land. He formed his own Soviet-style secret police organization, but his regime began to crumble when he failed to obtain Russian support after launching a series of attacks on Hungary's neighbors. Moreover, Kun's "Red" terrorism provoked a counter "White" terrorism organized by former Hungarian Army officers. Five months after

DANZIG AND THE POLISH CORRIDOR

The city of Danzig, Poland's most important Baltic seaport, has been a source of friction in Eastern Europe for centuries. Situated on an arm of the Vistula, it became an important commercial center after German merchants moved into the settlement in the 11th Century. Captured by the Teutonic Knights in the 14th Century, taken by Poland in the 15th, it became a part of Prussia in 1793 and remained almost uninterruptedly under Prussian control until the end of World War I. In 1919 the Allies, attempting to give Poland an outlet to the sea, made Danzig a "free city" and gave Poland access to it by a corridor some 20 to 90 miles wide which separated Germany from East Prussia. Poland's refusal to accede to Hitler's demand for the cession of Danzig and the creation of a German corridor across the Polish corridor precipitated World War II.

his dictatorship began he fled to the Soviet Union.

Admiral Miklós Horthy, former commander of the Habsburgs' Adriatic Fleet, became the new Hungarian leader in November 1919. To lend an aura of legality to the regime, Horthy's supporters asserted that Hungary was still part of the old Habsburg monarchy, and Horthy assumed the title of Regent. In fact he was to all purposes dictator of Hungary, and he was to remain so until after the outbreak of World War II.

Poland turned its attention toward strengthening its eastern frontiers against the threat presented by Bolshevik Russia. Piłsudski's first move after gathering together his scattered forces was to launch an offensive against the Russians. The Poles reached Kiev, but the Red Army was by no means defeated. It began a counterdrive toward Warsaw. With some staff aid from a small group of French officers, Piłsudski stopped the Russians outside Warsaw. The peace treaty which was finally signed at Riga in March 1921 led to the establishment of Poland's eastern boundary on a meandering line which took in both Wilno and Lwów.

THE new state was about half the size of the old Poland before the First Partition of 1772. Like Czechoslovakia, it contained a number of peoples of widely varying ethnic and cultural backgrounds. While some two million Poles were left outside the new frontiers, the population inside included some five million Ukrainians, a million Ruthenians and 800,000 Germans, as well as other minorities—some 30 per cent of the total population of 27 million. Jews constituted nearly 10 per cent of the population. Poland, mocked the Russians, was "the monstrous bastard of the Versailles Treaty."

The Europe of the Paris Peace Conference was indeed a strange child, concerning whose maintenance and education there were very different opinions. Preoccupied with its own postwar problems, the U.S. declined membership in the League of Nations, one of whose purposes was to guarantee the independence of the Polish and Czechoslovak republics. While Czechoslovakia remained a strong supporter of collective security, France and Britain placed their faith in a system of bilateral treaties. With the purpose of containing revolutionary Germany and

sealing off the Soviet Union, France made an alliance with Poland and fathered an alliance called the Little Entente between Czechoslovakia, Romania and Yugoslavia. The Russians scoffed at this group, but the Entente powers proved themselves effective in 1921 when ex-Emperor Charles and his wife Zita flew to Budapest and begged Admiral Horthy to live up to his title of Regent by giving Charles the Hungarian throne. With the Czechs and the Yugoslavs mobilizing half a million soldiers, the Hungarian Government promulgated a law barring the Habsburg succession for all time. Charles and Zita went off on a British destroyer to Madeira, where nine months later Charles, last of the Habsburgs to occupy a throne, died in despair.

The strength of the Western alliance, coupled with the failure of the German Communist revolution and the revival of German nationalism, led to a reversal of Soviet policy. At Rapallo, Italy, in 1922, the Russians signed a treaty with the counterrevolutionary German Government, and at home they embarked on a "New Economic Policy" of limited free enterprise. In 1924 Britain and France recognized the Soviet Union, and at Locarno, Switzerland, they signed a pact with Germany which guaranteed the borders of Belgium and France. With the Continent relatively stable at last, Eastern Europe breathed more easily.

For a time, there was progress. In Czechoslovakia a government of appointed officials was replaced by a parliamentary Cabinet headed by Beneš and then, as an increasing number of political parties appeared on the scene, by a series of coalition Cabinets. Because the Agrarian Party was in every Cabinet, agricultural policy received considerable attention. Large estates were expropriated and redistributed through the state Land Office. Other reforms were also undertaken. Hereditary titles were abolished, and social security was introduced.

IN Poland the Universities of Warsaw and Wilno were reopened, and new universities were founded at Lublin and Poznań. Free newspapers flourished, and a new literature blossomed. An eight-hour day and social security arrived; anti-Jewish legislation was repealed. Yet Poland remained a disunited society, its political parties unable to cooperate for the common good of the nation. In 1926 inflation swept the country. Some 300,000 men—20 per cent of the labor force—were out of work, and violent political demonstrations were organized by Socialist and Communist parties. "If there is one land in which an immediate revolutionary situation might crystallize in a comparatively short time it is Poland," observed Gregory Zinoviev, one of Josef Stalin's aides in the Soviet Union.

PILSUDSKI, who had retired in 1923, but who still enjoyed widespread support in the country, apparently agreed. In May 1926, with the aid of the Army and veterans of his famous legions, he carried out a coup d'état which forced the resignation of the Government. Once, during his guerrilla days in Russia, Piłsudski had said: "I have always had the impression that our national character lacks ruthlessness. That may be attractive, but is [of] damned little value in the world market. . . ." Now, at the age of 59, faced with the rapid decline of the country he loved, Piłsudski decided for ruthlessness. The results were not attractive. He put men he could trust—old cronies and veteran legionnaires—in responsible positions. Socialists and Communists were jailed. At the promised general elections in 1930 Piłsudski's men won by suspiciously large margins. A new constitution was drafted that greatly increased the powers of the presidency, an office which fell to a Piłsudski supporter, and decreased those of parliament. Economic conditions improved, and the internal Communist threat was averted, but Piłsudski died a tired and embittered old man in 1935, the progressive ideas of his youth only a memory. His authoritarian system was inherited by a military oligarchy which came to be known as "the regime of the colonels."

For many Europeans the years between 1920 and 1940 resemble an Alpine excursion by novice mountaineers: there is first the exhilarating ascent out of the valley of World War I, then a breathless pause at the summit and finally an uncontrolled, avalanche-like slide into World War II. In this figure of speech, there would be no difficulty identifying the summit as 1928 and 1929, the years before the world economic Depression hit Europe with full force. Between 1929 and 1933, for example, unemployment

in Czechoslovakia rose from 88,000 to almost one million.

Poland's exports dropped by two thirds, and working-class income declined 40 per cent. The Depression contributed to the rise of the National Radical Party (NARA) in Poland, and the Sudeten Party in Czechoslovakia, which was led by Konrad Henlein, a young gymnastics instructor. Henlein's group had connections with Adolf Hitler's National Socialist Party in Germany.

In Hungary there had been land reform of a kind: 1.3 million acres had been distributed, but not to those who most needed it. The Government of Admiral Horthy consisted of a coterie of landowners and gentry supported by businessmen and bureaucrats. As early as 1928 Hungary had found a friend in Mussolini, who that year had denounced the Trianon Treaty which had established Hungary's shrunken borders after the war. Heavily dependent on foreign credits and markets, Hungary was hard hit by the Depression. Its political as well as its economic stability was shaken, and a new, Right-Wing leader, Gyula Gömbös, a half-German anti-Semite, became Minister-President. On the election of Adolf Hitler in January 1933, Gömbös was among the first to offer congratulations.

In Poland Colonel Józef Beck, the Foreign Minister, lost no time in signing a nonaggression pact with Hitler. Poland's ally, France, which had not been consulted by Beck, responded by signing a separate pact of mutual assistance with Russia, as did Czechoslovakia, already allied with France. Poland thereupon renewed its nonaggression pact with the U.S.S.R.

YET these arrangements demanded firmness and strength on the part of national leaders if the aggressive drives of Nazi Germany under Adolf Hitler were to be halted; firmness and strength were not forthcoming. The Locarno treaties, which had guaranteed the frontiers of Germany, France and Belgium, were torn up when Hitler invaded the Rhineland unopposed in 1936. Germany's bloodless annexation of Austria followed. Then Hitler demanded the Sudetenland, a western strip of Czechoslovakia inhabited mostly by people of German origin, and threatened war unless what he called Germany's "last territorial claim" in Europe was met. Czechoslovakia was mobilized for war but left the decision to its allies. Russia said it would fight if France did; France said it would fight if Britain did; Britain suggested a conference. At Munich, on September 29, 1938, Prime Minister Neville Chamberlain of Britain and Premier Edouard Daladier of France told Hitler and Mussolini that they would not oppose the transfer of the Sudetenland to Germany. Returning to London Chamberlain waved a copy of the agreement, saying, "This is . . . peace with honor. I believe it is peace in our time."

Czechoslovakia's 40 crack divisions laid down their arms. A week after Munich Beneš, who had succeeded Masaryk in the presidency, resigned. Three weeks later he left Prague for London. Poland took the opportunity to seize that part of the Polish province of Teschen which had been ceded to Czechoslovakia at Versailles. Konrad Henlein's Sudeten Germans vociferously celebrated union with Nazi Germany. In March 1939 the Wehrmacht marched into Czechoslovakia, and a newly formed Czechoslovak Government was forced to sign a declaration making Bohemia and Moravia a German protectorate. Konstantin von Neurath, the German "Protector" of the region, began putting Nazi racial policies into effect. In reward for its support of Hitler, Hungary got back a large slice of Slovakia, which it had lost after World War I.

THIS, however, was not the end of German ambition in Eastern Europe. In March 1939 Hitler notified Poland that the Free City of Danzig must be handed over to Germany, and a few weeks later he denounced the German-Polish nonaggression treaty. On August 23 the Nazi-Soviet nonaggression pact was signed in Moscow. Although two days later Britain signed a mutual-assistance pact with Poland, the Nazis, seemingly released from the threat of Soviet interference, now thought themselves free to act as they wished in Eastern Europe.

On September 1, 1939, Germany invaded Poland. This was the first demonstration of Hitler's blitzkrieg tactics: thousands of motorized troops and tanks poured into Poland, preceded by coordinated air attacks. Two days after the invasion Britain and France declared war on Germany, but they could

not help the Poles. On September 17, while a desperate battle was being fought for Warsaw, the Russians invaded Poland from the east, in accordance with the terms of their pact with Germany. Members of the Polish Government fled. The Polish Army fought on for another 10 days, badly mauling the much-publicized Wehrmacht. No one knows how many Poles fell in battle, but 700,000 Polish prisoners are thought to have been taken by the Germans. The Russians captured 181,000 Polish soldiers and 10,000 officers. At the end of the fighting, Hitler appointed Dr. Hans Frank ruler of Poland with the title of Gauleiter. The Germans began carrying out Nazi racial policies immediately.

WHILE Poland was being brought to its knees, Beneš set up a Czechoslovak government-in-exile in London with Jan Masaryk, the late President's attractive and popular son, as Foreign Minister. At the same time Władysław Sikorski, a Polish general who had become the country's Premier on the outbreak of the war, arrived to set up a Polish government-in-exile. Sikorski hoped that Germany would immediately tangle with Russia, as had happened in World War I. But the Germans turned westward in May 1940 and swiftly overran the Low Countries and France. In June Charles de Gaulle arrived in London to set up a French government-in-exile. The following April Hitler invaded the Balkans, and soon there were other governments-in-exile. There was, however, no Hungarian refugee government. Hitler had offered Admiral Horthy a large slice of Yugoslavia containing some 500,000 ethnic Hungarians in return for the passage of German troops to the Balkans; Horthy agreed, and thus Hungary regained a substantial portion of the territory it had lost at the end of World War I. The country, however, did not fully commit itself to Hitler's cause; it permitted Polish airmen and soldiers who managed to cross into Hungary passage to the Free World.

Then Sikorski's hope came true. The friendship between Hitler and Stalin broke down when it became clear to both that neither would concede a paramount interest to the other in Eastern Europe and the Balkans. In June 1941 Hitler ordered the execution of long-developed plans for the invasion of Russia. Britain declared support for its new ally, but within three months the Soviet Army had been driven deep into Russia.

Silence covered Europe like a shroud. Boxcars of human freight were shunted from one country to another; in dark places prison camps spread like fungi. In the summer of 1942 Prime Minister Winston Churchill of Britain conferred with Stalin in Moscow and conceded that the Soviet Union had "a predominant interest" in Poland, Czechoslovakia and Hungary. Then, after the Russians had halted the Nazi advance at Stalingrad that winter, the Germans began to retreat along the 2,000-mile Russian front; Allied forces occupied North Africa and moved on to Italy. At Teheran, Iran, in December, the Big Three—Churchill, Roosevelt and Stalin—discussed the future of Europe and tentatively agreed that the new boundary between Poland and Russia should lie roughly on a north-south line approximately 100 miles east of Warsaw—the Curzon Line originally proposed as a basis for discussion at the Versailles conference by Lord Curzon, the British Foreign Minister. Marshal Piłsudski's successful invasion of Soviet Russia after World War I had rendered the suggestion meaningless at the time; the acceptance of the line by the Big Three meant that Poland would lose to Soviet Russia almost half the territory it had held between the wars.

THERE were other tragedies in store for Poland. In April 1943 the Russians refused a request from the London Poles for an International Red Cross investigation of a German report that the bodies of several thousand Polish officers, presumably those captured by the Russians in September 1939, had been found in mass graves in the Katyn Wood near Smolensk. The Russians first insisted that the Poles had been massacred by the Nazis; then they refused to permit an investigation. "Katyn Wood" became, to the Poles, a hated phrase; thereafter the Russians ignored the London Poles and created their own Polish Committee of National Liberation. Their intention of exercising their "predominant interest" in Poland became increasingly clear.

The Polish soldiers who had been captured by the Russians in 1939 had been placed under the command of the Polish General Władysław Anders (who had noted the absence of officers) and had been

promised equipment. When no equipment was forthcoming, they protested, and Stalin granted them permission to leave the country. With other Polish soldiers, sailors and airmen who had escaped after the 1939 debacle, they took part in a number of World War II engagements. The Poles also mustered a formidable underground Home Army of some 250,000 troops.

IN January 1944 the advancing Russians crossed the prewar boundary of Poland and established their Polish Committee of National Liberation in Lublin. Whenever they encountered elements of the Home Army the Russians arrested and imprisoned them or drafted them into the Red Army. The Red Army reached the outskirts of Warsaw in the fall of that year. Urged on by the Russians the Home Army launched an open offensive against the Germans inside the city. For two months the Russians remained nearby without firing a shot while the Germans destroyed the Home Army. Only then did the Red Army attack and take the city. The following January the Russians recognized the Lublin committee as the provisional government of Poland and its head, Bolesław Bierut, a Moscow-trained Communist, as Premier.

Katyn Wood and the refusal of the Russians to aid the Home Army underlined Soviet intransigence toward Poland. The case of Czechoslovakia was different. The bitter taste of Munich had caused the Czech government-in-exile to lean toward Moscow. President Beneš first talked to Vyacheslav Molotov, the Soviet Foreign Minister, about a future Polish-Czech federation, but, receiving no encouragement, advanced the idea of a future Czechoslovakia made ethnically homogeneous by the expulsion of minorities. The Russians accepted this idea. A few days after the Big Three meeting at Teheran Beneš signed a Friendship Pact with Russia.

Hungary would have welcomed an Allied drive through the Balkans in its direction; no such offensive was undertaken, however, and when Hitler lost faith in Horthy's loyalty early in 1944 the German Army occupied the country. As the Soviet Army approached Hungary, Horthy contacted Moscow but was seized by the Nazis and forced to abdicate. In January 1945 a provisional government of Hungary signed an armistice, and in April the German and Hungarian armies were driven into Austria by the Soviet advance.

The Big Three met at Yalta in the Crimea on February 4, 1945, three months before the war ended in Europe. They confirmed the Curzon Line as the new Polish-Soviet border. In an effort to avoid a break with Stalin, Roosevelt and Churchill also agreed to recognize the committee the Russians had established in Lublin as the provisional government of Poland, although they insisted that it include democratic Polish leaders and that the new government hold "free and unfettered elections. . . ." The Russians implemented the agreement by inviting 16 leaders of the Home Army to Moscow, where they were promptly jailed. At the same time the Russians accepted Stanisław Mikołajczyk, who had become chief of the London Poles, as a member of the "Government of National Unity," the new title of the Lublin group. The U.S. and Britain thereupon withdrew recognition of the London government-in-exile.

A T the conference of Allied powers in Potsdam, Germany, in the summer of 1945, it was decided that Poland should be given some compensation for the loss of its eastern territories to the Soviet Union. Its western border was accordingly established on the Oder and Neisse Rivers. This gave the country some 39,400 square miles of former German territory. The estimated two million Germans still east of the Oder-Neisse border were to be deported westward to make way for an estimated 4.5 million Poles who would move from what would now be Soviet lands east of the Curzon Line. Actually, many Poles remained in their old homes, and some 3.5 million Poles were settled in Poland's new western territories.

Once established, the new National Unity Government nationalized larger industries, abolished the senate and promulgated a new electoral bill barring collaborators and alleged collaborators from voting; it did not collectivize the land for fear of causing a peasant upheaval. But the Communists were in control. In 1946 the party announced that its membership had increased from 20,000 to 364,000. In the general election in January 1947 Mikołajczyk's Peasant Party, which was the most popular party in

Poland, won only 28 out of 444 seats because of brutal police intimidation of voters. The new parliament elected Bolesław Bierut President of Poland. With the last hope of a democratic Poland gone, Mikołajczyk fled the country.

T HE Communists proceeded somewhat differently in Czechoslovakia. The Soviet Army had liberated Slovakia in March 1945, and a provisional government called the National Front was set up. Beneš became President; Zdeněk Fierlinger, the Communist-leaning Social Democratic Party leader, was named Premier; and Jan Masaryk took the post of Foreign Minister. Key positions in the Cabinet were taken by Communists. As the Soviet Army advanced into the country, National Committees led by Czech Communists who had been trained in Russia during the war were set up in every district to take over the functions of local government. On May 10 the populace, half-demented with joy, welcomed Beneš and Jan Masaryk to Prague.

Both had placed much store in popular support. But the Communists had plans of their own. An atmosphere of suspicion and fear was created by local Communist Party committees which denounced anyone they regarded as a "class enemy." Some 300,000 non-Communists were struck off the electoral rolls as "suspected" collaborators. Many real collaborators joined the Communist Party, whose membership climbed rapidly.

In the general election of May 1946 the Communists polled 38 per cent of the vote, and Klement Gottwald, the leader of the Czech Communist Party, became Premier in a coalition Cabinet composed of Communists, Beneš' National Socialists and other parties. The Communists took the key ministries, including Interior (police) and Information (radio and newspapers). They demanded nationalization of industry and collectivization of the land, but the National Socialists held out for limited "private sectors" in both. The question was somewhat academic; the real issue dividing Beneš and the Communists was whether Czechoslovakia would remain free or fall under complete Soviet domination.

As the 1948 general election approached, the Communists launched a press and radio campaign of unprecedented calumny against National Socialist leaders. There were attempts to assassinate non-Communist Cabinet members; when it was discovered that Communists were behind the attempts the Communist-dominated police took no action. The Cabinet ordered an inquiry. When Gottwald failed to carry out the investigation, non-Communist members of the Cabinet, hoping to topple the Gottwald Government, submitted their resignations to President Beneš. Gottwald, however, was prepared for such a move. Arms were distributed to Communist groups, mass meetings of workers were convened, and factories were taken over by workers' militia. Valerian Zorin, Deputy Foreign Minister of the Soviet Union, flew in from Moscow, a reminder to Beneš that the U.S.S.R. stood solidly behind the Czech Communists. Denied access even to the Communist-controlled radio, Beneš was helpless; he accepted the proffered resignations, and on February 25, 1948, approved a new Cabinet list supplied by Gottwald and made up of Communists and pro-Communists. On March 10 Jan Masaryk was found dead in the courtyard of the Foreign Office; it was widely believed that he had been defenestrated. Three months later Beneš resigned the presidency. It was the final curtain fall for Czech democracy.

FOR 17 years Beneš had been Foreign Minister of Czechoslovakia and for 11 years its President; he had played a unique part in the history of Eastern Europe. Almost the final sentence of his memoirs reads: "I believe that peaceful cooperation between [Communism and democracy] is possible and that it is right and necessary." On the eve of the February 1948 coup d'état he revised his view. "I know them, these people in Moscow," he told a trusted aide. "You overestimate their intelligence and their farsightedness. I overestimated them too. They understand nothing of other countries. They take themselves for realists: at bottom they are only fanatics. Their whole policy is a provocation to war. They will pay dearly for it. They are as blind as Hitler. . . . Like Hitler they will suffer the consequences." Three months later Beneš was dead.

The Communist take-over technique varied in each country in accordance, apparently, with the Russians' judgment of conditions. In Poland the Communists did not bother to conceal the iron fist of Soviet power; in Czechoslovakia they pulled on the glove of legality; in Hungary they employed first the fist, then the glove. Although Hungary was ostensibly governed by an Allied Control Commission composed of British, American and Soviet representatives, it was actually under the control of the occupying Soviet Army at the war's end. The country was pillaged, forced to pay an indemnity of $300 million and required to feed the Soviet troops. Thousands of political leaders and civilians were deported to Russia as "prisoners of war," a move calculated to terrify the populace.

THE elections of 1945, however, were free, and the Smallholders, the predominant party of small businessmen and landholders, won an absolute majority. Yielding to Soviet pressure, they granted the Communists representation in the Cabinet. But as the major impediment in the Communist path, the Smallholders rapidly became the party's prime target. Early in 1946 a number of Smallholder deputies were persuaded by the Communists to form a rival party. Many members of the Smallholders bitterly criticized the policies of their leader, Prime Minister Ferenc Nagy, who, however, felt that he had to placate the Communists as long as Soviet forces were occupying the country.

At the end of the year the Communists accused the Government of laying plans to restore Admiral Horthy to power. The Communist-controlled police then arrested many Smallholders, including Béla Kovács, the Smallholders' Secretary-General, on charges of reactionary conspiracy. The following May Prime Minister Nagy, on vacation in Switzerland, was accused of similar activities, together with many of his deputies. A number of them fled the country; Nagy did not return from Switzerland. There was little point; the Communists took another year to destroy the remaining non-Communist parties, but the hope of freedom was gone in Hungary.

For Eastern Europe the gates had closed again. More than once during the war Churchill had noted that Stalin wished to establish Soviet hegemony over the region. In 1946 he confirmed that observation in a famous phrase: "From Stettin in the Baltic to Trieste in the Adriatic, an iron curtain has descended across the continent."

FOUNDERS OF A NATION, Czech and Slovak patriots led by Thomas Masaryk *(seated, center),* who became the first President of Czechoslovakia, gather in 1918 before the Liberty Bell in Philadelphia to dramatize their demands for independence. The Allies sponsored the new nation, in part because of aid given by Czechs and Slovaks to their cause during World War I.

A Turbulent Entrance into the Modern World

The Eastern Europe of today was created by swift power shifts and diplomatic jockeying at the end of World War I. The Allies, committed to the destruction of the Austro-Hungarian Empire, sponsored national independence for the Czechs and Slovaks under the leadership of Thomas Masaryk. Hungary, which had fought on the side of the Central Powers as a part of the empire, became independent but quickly fell under a dictatorship. The Polish nationalist Józef Piłsudski won considerable territory for his country by a postwar invasion of revolutionary Russia; then Poland, too, lapsed into dictatorship. In the next two decades Russia gathered strength and Hitler's Germany began to rearm. Caught between the two giants, the Eastern European nations sought security in alliances: Czechoslovakia with Russia and France, Poland with England and France, Hungary with Germany. The futility of these pacts became clear when the Allies gave Hitler much of Czechoslovakia at Munich. Soon Germany invaded Poland. There was an atmosphere of hope when the war ended, but in a few years Russia won control of all of Eastern Europe.

HUNGARIAN COMMUNIST, Béla Kun, who became the country's President in 1919, greets supporters in Budapest. During his five-month regime Kun tried to nationalize all industry.

LEADER OF A COUP, Admiral Miklós Horthy of Hungary salutes from a carriage. He overthrew Kun in 1919 and remained the country's strongest figure until the end of World War II.

POLISH STRONG MAN, General Józef Piłsudski proceeds through Warsaw in 1919 with the pianist Ignace Jan Paderewski, who was then the country's Premier. In 1921 Piłsudski resigned as chief of state when a new constitution limited his powers, but in 1926 he instituted a military coup and ruled until his death in 1935. Another military regime followed Piłsudski's.

MANEUVERING by anxious leaders in the years before World War II failed to halt the Nazi war machine

FORMING AN ALLIANCE in 1935, Foreign Minister Eduard Beneš of Czechoslovakia *(left)* and Soviet Foreign Minister Maxim Litvinov *(center)* sign a mutual-security pact in Moscow. Czechoslovakia sought protection from Hitler's Germany.

GIVING THE NAZI SALUTE, thousands of Germans demonstrate in the Czechoslovakian Sudetenland in 1938. Blatantly encouraged by Nazi Germany, such rallies lent propagandistic weight to Adolf Hitler's claims that the region should be made a part of Germany. At Munich, in 1938, the Sudetenland was handed over to the Nazis in a vain effort to appease Hitler.

BIDDING FAREWELL to Chancellor Hitler in 1941, Admiral Horthy of Hungary waves from a train departing Germany. As an ally of Hitler, Hungary participated in the invasion of neighboring Yugoslavia and in the campaign against Russia.

ENTERING WARSAW, German troops complete the conquest of Poland *(below)*. Forty-four German divisions moved into Poland on September 1, 1939, and crushed the nation within a month—but the fighting cost the invaders some 12,000 deaths.

IN PURPOSEFUL LINE, Soviet troops reach the outskirts of Warsaw in 1944. They delayed entering the city proper for months while the Polish underground army, which rose against the Nazis, was slaughtered.

DISMAYED PATRIOT, Stanisław Mikołajczyk fled to England in 1947 soon after his Peasant Party had been badly defeated in that year's Polish elections because of Communist intimidation of the voters.

UNDERMINED by Communist maneuvering, postwar governments were swiftly taken over by the forces of the far Left

NATIONAL LEADERS, President Eduard Beneš *(seated)* and Foreign Minister Jan Masaryk confer in Prague in 1947. After a Communist coup in February 1948 Masaryk was found dead.

AGING PRESIDENT, Eduard Beneš announces to the Communist Prime Minister Klement Gottwald *(right)* that he will accept the resignation of non-Communist Cabinet ministers.

MOURNING FRIENDS attend the last rites for Jan Masaryk in Prague. Beneš sits slumped in despair at center. After the February coup the Communists purged all opposition and placed scores of opponents under temporary arrest. Beneš himself resigned from the presidency in June rather than sign a new Communist constitution, and died three months later.

MEMORIAL TO HORROR, a relief marks the site of the
Warsaw Ghetto into which Polish Jews were herded. In 1942
some 500,000 Jews lived in the Ghetto; 200 survived the war.

DEATH FACTORY at Auschwitz, Poland, stands desolate today *(left)*. In this camp the Nazis killed some four million people by gassing, injections of poison, hanging or shooting.

Aging Josef Cardinal Beran, prohibited from functioning as Roman Catholic Primate of Czechoslovakia since 1949, walks on an estate near

Prague where he lived after his release from close confinement in 1963.

5

In the Grip of Communism

WHEN the Communists established themselves in control of Eastern Europe they fully realized that more than one obstacle stood in the path of bringing Poland, Czechoslovakia and Hungary into the Marxist paradise. The brutality and cynicism of their seizure of power had engendered widespread hate and fear of them; moreover, religion, with its innate hostility to Marxist materialism, was strong throughout the area. Religious faith itself, the Communists believed, might take generations to destroy; they therefore turned their primary energies to bringing the Churches to heel in order to eliminate them as potential rallying centers for resistance to their regimes. Inevitably their major target was the Roman Catholic Church, strongest of the faiths in Eastern Europe.

In Poland more than 95 per cent of the population professed Catholicism, and there the Communists at first trod with extreme care. They exempted Church lands from seizure when land reform was undertaken in 1944, and they offered state aid in rebuilding the hundreds of churches that had been damaged during the war. But the conciliatory tactics did not last long. In September 1945 the Communist-controlled Government denounced the Concordat signed in 1925 between the Vatican and the Polish Government on the grounds that the Vatican had appointed German priests to Polish dioceses during World War II and had not yet recognized the new Communist Government of postwar Poland. Restrictions were then gradually applied to Church religious-instruction programs and to the functions and privileges of religious orders. In March 1950 the Government took the drastic step of confiscating virtually all lands belonging to the Church.

THESE assaults, and an increasingly vehement propaganda campaign directed against both Church and clergy, made the Polish bishops anxious to reach some sort of compromise with the Government. In April 1950 the Polish bishops agreed to call upon Catholics to cooperate fully with the Government's reconstruction and welfare programs, to instruct the clergy to preach respect for state authority, and to be guided by the Polish national interest alone—except in matters of faith, morals and Church government. The bishops also agreed to press the Holy See to set up a permanent Church administration in the new western territories which Poland had acquired from Germany at the end of World War II. Such an action, the Communists realized, would constitute tacit recognition by the Vatican that the former German territories now belonged to Poland. In return for these commitments the Government agreed, among other things, to cease placing restrictions on religious education. The Communists regarded the Church's concessions merely as levers with which to apply further pressure.

The Vatican, however, did not take immediate action. Six months after the Church-state agreement had been signed, the Polish Government served notice that it would not wait much longer for recognition of the new boundaries, and in January 1951 it announced the "liquidation" of the temporary Church administrative system in the western territories. Acting in accordance with canon law, Church councils in each of the western dioceses thereupon elected priests to replace the ousted provisional administrators, and Archbishop Stefan Wyszyński, the

Primate of Poland, rapidly approved their selections. The continuity of Church administration had been preserved, but the Government had shown its power to interfere with Church appointments.

It was by no means finished exercising that power. The Government had earlier begun to arrest and try priests on charges of "antistate" activity; it now stepped up that program. In many parishes imprisoned priests were replaced by others willing to collaborate. Early in 1953 the Government again struck at the Church with a decree asserting its right to pass on the fitness of clergymen for Church office. The decree also demanded that all Church appointees swear an oath of loyalty to the Polish People's Republic, and stated that any member of the Church hierarchy found guilty of activities against "law or public order" would be removed from his position.

Shortly thereafter a show trial was staged to prove the charge that the entire Polish episcopate was subversive. The trial featured a bishop, three priests and a nun. After the bishop, who had been imprisoned for more than two years, had "confessed" that he had obeyed the German occupation authorities and that he had enjoyed friendly relations with the U.S. Embassy in the postwar years, the entire group received heavy prison sentences. Wyszyński, who had been appointed a cardinal in the interim, had strongly protested the trial and the sentences, and a few weeks later he was arrested. His incarceration was not the capstone to the campaign against the Church; by the beginning of 1954 several hundred Polish priests and nine bishops had been imprisoned.

IN Hungary the Communist assault on the Church was much more direct. There, Roman Catholics comprised 60 per cent of the population at the end of World War II. Premier Mátyás Rákosi, the most ruthless of Moscow's satraps in Eastern Europe, was not troubled by that. Rákosi had, in fact, been scornful of the Polish Communists for what he considered their hesitant, gradualist approach with the Church. He boasted of having told the Poles that "the way they were doing it was wrong. They must do it my way—arrest one church dignitary and bribe the rest, and that's all there is to it."

In February 1949 Rákosi acted on his own advice and ordered the arrest of Jozsef Cardinal Mindszenty,

Primate of the Hungarian Catholic Church. Mindszenty was given a show trial at which he confessed to a fantastic array of charges. Sentenced to life imprisonment, Mindszenty became a martyr to the Hungarians, and in demonstration of their hatred of the regime they flocked to the churches in evergreater numbers. The Government was prepared to deal with that; it turned to mass arrests and trials of priests. Then, after an unsuccessful attempt to create a collaborationist faction within the Church, it established an Office of Church Affairs which began openly interfering in Church administration. Arrests continued; in May 1951 Jozsef Grösz, Archbishop of Kalocsa, was sentenced to life imprisonment. After that, members of the AVH, the Communist secret police, were appointed as diocesan "advisers." They had power to order the transfer of priests to remote villages and to remove priests who became too popular with their parishioners. Similar repressive measures were applied to the Protestant denominations and the surviving Jewish congregations.

IN Czechoslovakia, where about 75 per cent of the people were Roman Catholics, the Communists followed a seemingly conciliatory policy toward the Church after the February 1948 coup which brought them to power. While seizing Church lands and schools they professed good will; as late as June, while negotiations on Church-state relations were being carried on, the country's leading Communists attended a Mass celebrated by then-Archbishop Josef Beran in Prague.

When the negotiations reached an impasse early in 1949, however, the Government launched an all-out campaign. Its first move was to dissolve Catholic Action, a society of priests and laymen, and to replace it with a new organization led by "patriotic" priests. Archbishop Beran and all of the country's bishops were placed under surveillance and later under house arrest. The public reading of pastoral letters without Government consent was prohibited.

Then, in October 1949, a State Office for Church Affairs was established and charged with central authority over all Churches and religious institutions. Clergymen went on the state payroll at a base salary of $750 a year, and although they were ostensibly recognized as Church employees they were required to meet the same employment standards as Government employees.

In February 1950 the Roman Catholic bishops refused to take a newly instituted oath of loyalty to the Communist regime, although they permitted the lower clergy to do so. This time the Government struck back in earnest. Seminaries and monasteries were shut down. Mass arrests and trials of priests on charges of espionage and conspiracy followed. Archbishop Beran was banished from Prague, and many of the higher Church dignitaries were given prison sentences. By April 1951 seven of the 12 Czechoslovak bishops had taken the loyalty oath. The era of open resistance by the Church had ended.

Religion was not, of course, the only institution against which the Communists moved in Eastern Europe. They took action on cultural and economic fronts as well (see Chapter 9), and the haste and crudity which marked their actions generated resentment even among some members of the local Communist hierarchy. The policies which were applied in the socialization of the area were dictated directly by Moscow, and the Eastern European leaders were granted no scope to adapt the general line to national differences prevailing in each country. Soviet dictates were accompanied by Soviet economic exploitation, and many Communists in Eastern Europe chafed under the excessiveness of Soviet control. A turning point came in 1948 when Yugoslavia broke away from the Soviet orbit to develop its own Communist society. To circumvent further defections, Stalin ordered a widespread purge of satellite Communists who might be suspected of nationalist tendencies.

THE most elaborately staged trial of the entire Stalin era was held in Budapest in September 1949 to lend substance to an omnibus series of charges against former Interior Minister Lászlo Rajk, one of the men who had been instrumental in achieving Communist control of Hungary. A series of witnesses, who all later disappeared or were given prison sentences, was brought into court to confirm Rajk's "confession" that he had been a spy for Admiral Horthy, the German Gestapo, the Deuxième Bureau (France's intelligence agency), the U.S.'s Office of Strategic Services (the World War II forerunner of the C.I.A.) and Yugoslavia. Rajk, a tough veteran of the Spanish Civil War who had been interned in France and had spent some time in a Nazi concentration camp during World War II, had been persuaded by János Kádár, his successor as Interior Minister, to confess to save his life. A few weeks after the trial he was hanged.

On the heels of Rajk's execution came a wave of arrests of "reactionary elements" and members of the democratic political parties that had been dissolved in Hungary when the Communists took over. Hungarian Communists who had not undergone training in Moscow, and were therefore regarded with suspicion by the Kremlin, were next to be purged. Kádár himself, a non-Muscovite, was purged, tortured and imprisoned.

The Yugoslav breakaway had repercussions in Poland as well. Władysław Gomułka was dismissed from his post as Secretary-General of the Polish Communist Party in September 1948. The reasons were obvious. Gomułka had had the temerity to defend the Yugoslavs, albeit guardedly, and to question the wisdom of their abrupt expulsion by Stalin from the Cominform, an organization set up in 1947 to facilitate Soviet control of the infant "people's democracies." Gomułka was charged with having been a "nationalist deviationist." He had in fact stressed the need for a distinctly "Polish road to Socialism" since shortly after his assumption of the leadership of the Polish party in 1943. He was accused, in addition, of harboring a defiant attitude toward the Soviet Union, of seeking to gain absolute power within the party and of having attempted to sabotage the collectivization of agriculture. Gomułka was expelled from the Central Committee in 1949 and was eventually placed under house arrest. In the witch hunt that accompanied his fall almost one quarter of the members of the party were expelled.

CZECHOSLOVAKIA, too, felt the force of anti-Yugoslav repression. With Stalin's backing, President Klement Gottwald removed Rudolf Slánský from the secretary-generalship of the Czech Communist Party in September 1951. In a 1952 trial, whose list of charges echoed the indictment lodged against László Rajk of Hungary three years earlier, but which contained overtones of anti-Semitism in addition, Slánský was accused of being a Zionist, a Yugoslav agent, a tool of the "imperialist agent Beneš" and a U.S. spy. He confessed and was hanged.

The purges halted abruptly with Stalin's death in March 1953. While a new struggle for power took place within the Kremlin walls the one-man leadership and the "cult of personality" of Stalin's era were denounced by Russia's new collective leadership. Collective leadership became fashionable in Eastern Europe, too. As in the Soviet Union, the secret police were curbed; many men who had been imprisoned during the Stalin era were quietly released. Among them were victims of the purge trials, like Kádár and Gomułka. Efforts were made to rehabilitate the agricultural and consumer-goods sectors of the economies, which had been severely crippled during the all-out drive for industrialization ordered by Stalin. The general easing of controls encouraged writers and intellectuals to begin open criticism of the regimes' shortcomings.

THERE were other surprises to come. In 1955 Nikita Khrushchev and Nikolai Bulganin, the new Soviet leaders, journeyed to Belgrade to tender public apologies to Marshal Tito, Yugoslavia's leader, for the harsh treatment Stalin had given him. With this act Tito's national Communism was suddenly given the stamp of respectability.

Then, in 1956, the Communist world was shaken to its foundations. News leaked out of Khrushchev's secret speech to the Soviet Party Congress in February. In the speech he had cited a lengthy roster of Stalin's crimes, carefully selected to avoid touching upon wrongs done to Eastern Europe. More than a few Eastern European Communists and non-Communists began to draw comparisons between Stalin's behavior and that of their own Communist bosses. In Eastern Europe, furthermore, the comparisons did not halt at condemnations of particular persons or circumstances. A basic questioning of the entire Communist system began.

Even the relatively docile Czechs became restive; they were, however, easily cowed when the local Communist hierarchy launched a resolute attack against any demands for major liberalization. But by the summer of 1956 Poland and Hungary rumbled with change and bold demands for drastic reforms.

SIMPLE CRUCIFIX stands in a quiet cemetery in Zakopane, Poland, where many members of prominent families of the Tatra mountain area are buried. In an apparent effort to stylize his work, the wood carver placed a smock over Christ's torso.

The Church: Former Ally and Contemporary Victim

For centuries state and Church were close allies in Eastern Europe. Today religion is the state's victim. In Czechoslovakia many priests and bishops are kept under house arrest, and Roman Catholic publications are forbidden. Although 60 per cent of the people were born to Catholic parents, services are attended mostly by the old. Judaism once flourished in Prague, but there and in the rest of Eastern Europe it will never recover from the extermination of millions of Jews by the Nazis. While religion has suffered considerably in Czechoslovakia, the Communists have been less successful in Hungary; in spite of the disbanding of religious orders, the devout Hungarians continue to attend services. A significantly large Protestant movement holds its own as well. In Poland, which is overwhelmingly Roman Catholic, religion plays a major national role. Led by Stefan Cardinal Wyszyński, the Church is vocal and influential—despite Government threats to impose heavy taxes on Church properties and revenues.

89

INTENT PRIEST hears a confession as the faithful wait a turn near the Jasna Góra monastery at Częstochowa. In 1655 the monastery became a rallying point of resistance against invaders. Poles have made pilgrimages here ever since.

GOTHIC CHAPEL stands inside the Częstochowa basilica, which was built about 1690 to replace the monastery's original wooden church. Poland has been a devoutly Roman Catholic country ever since King Mieszko was converted in 966 and permitted German missionaries to preach Catholicism.

HOLY MASS for pilgrims to Częstochowa is offered beneath a revered portrait of the Virgin entitled *The Black Madonna.* By legend painted by St. Luke the Evangelist, it is possibly the work of an unknown 14th Century Italian artist.

CONFERRING HIS BLESSINGS, Stefan Cardinal Wyszyński meets well-wishers outside the Częstochowa monastery. Every year he presides over the gathering of pilgrims at the monastery.

MEDITATING, Cardinal Wyszyński prepares to speak to the crowd at Częstochowa. A forthright prelate, he has long been one of the most powerful Roman Catholic leaders in the region.

PRONOUNCING A BENEDICTION on the throng of thousands, Cardinal Wyszyński *(at center, wearing miter)* brings the annual events at Częstochowa to a climax. Although the Church in Poland has lost many privileges, its prestige remains high. More than 90 per cent of the Poles are Catholics, and the younger generation shows no sign of abandoning the faith.

EXQUISITE DECORATION in the old churches recalls an era when religion was a prospering, powerful force

DRAMATIC ALTAR in the 15th Century Matthias Church in Gyöngyöspata, Hungary, is set off by a lofty backdrop of gilded carvings of saints ascending toward a Virgin and Child.

TREASURED PAINTING of the Virgin and Child, one of the many masterpieces at the Oliwa Cathedral in Danzig, Poland, shines in the light of two tall candles.

RELIGIOUS EMBLEMS on a wall of the Oliwa Cathedral show wood carving at its finest. At the top is an elaborate clock which has an angel to strike the hours.

OPULENT CHAPEL in Karlštejn Castle in Czechoslovakia, built by the Holy Roman Emperor Charles IV about 1350, is adorned with carved semiprecious stones and sacred paintings.

EMBELLISHED PORTRAIT in the Oliwa Cathedral shows a Virgin and Child (left) in robes and crowns of gold, which were added long after the execution of the original painting.

JUDAISM, once the faith of millions in the region, today survives in an atmosphere of sorrow and age

DRAPED LECTERN, on which Old Testament Scriptures rest for reading during services, is the focal point for the peaceful interior of the Old-New Synagogue in Prague. Built in 1270, this is the oldest synagogue still in use in Eastern Europe.

CLOSELY GROUPED HEADSTONES in the cemetery of the Prague Ghetto *(opposite)* mark the graves of almost 200,000 Jews who died between 1439 and 1787. The Prague Ghetto was once a center of Jewish cultural activity in Eastern Europe.

PENSIVE WORSHIPER stands in the Old-New Synagogue under a drapery *(right)* which covers the Ark, repository of the sacred books between services. Before the Nazi anti-Semitic campaigns one third of Europe's Jews lived in Eastern Europe.

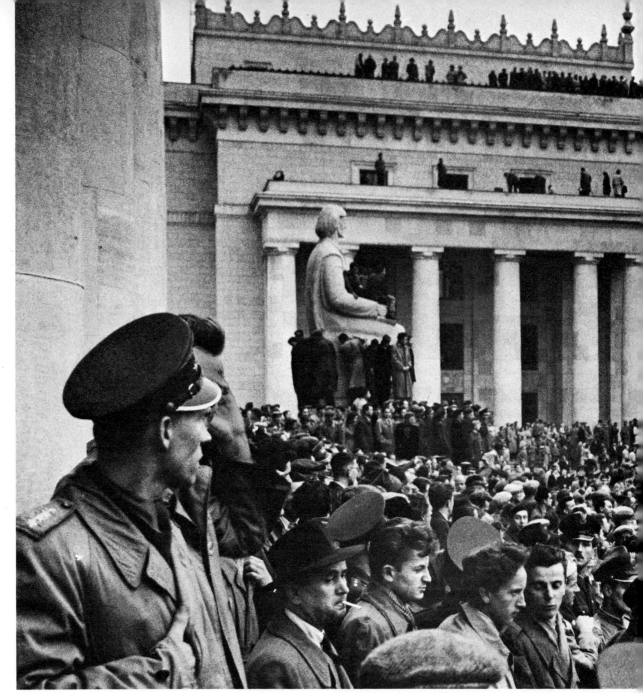

A crowd of several hundred thousand Poles gathers in Warsaw on October 24, 1956, to cheer Władysław Gomułka, new chief of the

Warsaw the Defiant

Polish party. Condemned as a "nationalist" during the Stalin era, he was restored to power as the country seethed under Soviet domination.

"THE cradle of Slavdom" was a title bestowed by 19th Century Pan-Slav enthusiasts on the High Tatra mountain range. Next to the High Tatra rises the Beskid range, source of the river Vistula that flows through the heart of Poland. It is not difficult to imagine primitive European man crossing the 7,000-foot fastness of the High Tatra or slowly venturing down the Vistula, forming settlements at those convenient points above flood level which are now the cities of Cracow, Warsaw, Toruń and Danzig. A second great river, the Oder, also rises in the same region. Flowing in a northwesterly direction, it is joined by a tributary from the south, the Neisse. The river then descends into the Baltic Sea north of the town of Stettin (Szczecin). Together the Oder and the Neisse Rivers form the western frontier of Poland established at the end of World War II—the so-called Oder-Neisse line. Much of the agricultural wealth of Poland is produced on the undulating plains which form the watershed of these two river systems, now linked by a canal.

At the foot of the Tatra sits Cracow, the largest Polish city to retain its historic aspect. The fortifications that once surrounded the ancient town walls have been replaced by a pleasant, tree-shaded walk; inside the walls, there is an enchanting jumble of medieval houses surrounding a wide square at the center of which is the Cloth Hall, a market dating from the 14th Century. The city is filled with museums and galleries which possess many notable works of art. Italian Renaissance merges happily with Gothic on the Wawel, a hill on the bend of the Vistula where the ancient kings of Poland built a royal palace and a cathedral in which a number of them lie beneath chiseled marble. Marshal Józef Piłsudski is also buried here. The royal palace is one of the show places of Poland. In it the visitor, wearing the felt slippers which are mandatory in all Polish museums, passes softly through a series of princely rooms paved and decorated in colored marbles and hung with superb Flemish tapestries. In one room there is a ceiling into which realistic heads of medieval officials have been carved; they give a wonderful sense of the people of those times. During World War II Cracow was the command post of the Gestapo and the administrative headquarters of Dr. Hans Frank, one of whose first acts as Nazi Gauleiter of Poland was to send the entire faculty of the Jagiełłonian University to concentration camps.

Outside the walls of Old Cracow, there is a modern complex of factories and sprawling housing developments. Its center is the Nowa Huta steel plant, built after World War II. But industry is not new to this region. Archeologists recently unearthed traces of an iron foundry dating from the Fourth Century.

Driving westward from Cracow toward Katowice is like driving through western Pennsylvania; the sky is a tawny pall of smoke from coke ovens and gasworks; railroads push everywhere. The Germans chose the region as the site of the more infamous of

---

POLAND: SOME BASIC FACTS

AREA: 120,733 square miles

POPULATION: 29,731,000

MONETARY UNIT: The zloty (valued at $.25 at the official exchange rate, about $.04 at the more realistic tourist rate). This book employs the official rate except when noted.

MAJOR EXPORTS: Machinery, fuels, minerals, metals, food

RELIGIONS: Roman Catholic, Orthodox, Protestant

---

their extermination centers: Auschwitz, Birkenau and Dwory. With grass growing over the crumbling masonry of the former crematories, the uncompleted "boiling-down" works and the pyre pits, it is hard to realize that four million people died here. The visitor can still see the double fence of posts curved like hockey sticks; empty cylinders of Cyclon B, the swift-acting gas that was used to asphyxiate masses of people locked into airtight rooms; and piles of human hair, clothes and eyeglasses which the Nazis salvaged from the dead. A less blatant reminder of the Nazi presence is a quiet pool mirroring speckled birch trees into which the ashes of the dead were dumped.

Galicia—southeast Poland—has a Gothic flavor. If the visitor ignores the vacation hotels, hydroelectric plants and natural-gas pipelines, he will discover a wild, mountainous country covered with fir forests and intersected by small, angry torrents. There are trout in the streams and otters on their banks; there are black storks, cranes, minks and martens in the region. The nonvenomous aesculapian snake—original of the doctor's symbol—is indigenous.

Hitler had a secret redoubt built near the Galician town of Krosno. In it he entertained Mussolini in 1941, and from it he directed the opening stages of the war against the Soviet Union. In 1944, when the Soviet Army broke into this region, the Germans strongly fortified and mined the Dukla Pass, the route to Czechoslovakia. Soviet infantry stormed the Nazi positions and, after very heavy fighting, broke through. So many died on both sides that the place is now frequently referred to as "The Pass of the Dead."

The Soviet breakthrough is held to be the reason why neither Cracow nor Lublin was destroyed; another cause may have been the fact that the S.S. took to its heels, no member of that elite corps wishing to be caught near Auschwitz or Majdanek. Lying just east of Lublin, Majdanek was an extermination center where the Nazis experimented with execution techniques; eventually they killed some 1.5 million people there, including many Greeks, Czechs and French. The old town of Lublin remains in good shape, full of 16th Century Gothic monuments.

If the visitor prefers the florid architectural style of baroque, there is Częstochowa, an industrial town about 50 miles north of Katowice. Here on the Jasna Góra (Mountain of Light) is the monastery of the Pauline Fathers. It dates from 1382 but was re-fashioned in baroque in the 17th Century. The monastery's most revered possession is *The Black Madonna,* a portrait which tradition says was painted by St. Luke the Evangelist. In 1655, when the Swedes overran Poland, they besieged the monastery, but it is said that when the abbot held up *The Black Madonna* the Swedes turned and ran. This was the beginning of the end of the Swedish invasion. Jasna Góra is today the holiest of Polish shrines, and every August 100,000 pilgrims come to see *The Black Madonna.* In its publications the Government states that the portrait is "in reality the work of an unknown Italian artist of the Siena school," and in 1963 it tried to ban the pilgrimage on the ground that there was a smallpox epidemic in the region. Many thousands of people nevertheless visited Jasna Góra that year. The smallpox scare simply improved the medieval atmosphere of the occasion.

TRAVELING west from Częstochowa the visitor soon enters the new "western territories," which were formerly a part of Germany. Although the inhabitants are uniformly Polish, the countryside —with its tidy farms, neat villages and spired churches—looks German. At Wrocław (the former Breslau, noted for its churches and musicians), there was desperate fighting at the end of World War II, and only a skeleton remained of the old city—whose streets, one Western observer remarked, were "terrifying canyons running through silent walls of gutted houses." Wrocław is still a sad city, although the Poles have removed millions of tons of rubble, built some 68,000 housing units and reconstructed the old city square.

Macabre reminders of World War II are constantly turning up in the western territories. A few years ago men working in a forest near the town of Zagań, not far from Wrocław, uncovered a mass grave near a smaller one which had contained the remains of 50 British RAF men who had been among the 76 fliers who managed a mass break from Stalag VIII-C in March 1944. An investigating commission discovered other mass graves in an area of about 40 acres around Zagań; an estimated 40,000 Allied prisoners of war were said to have been buried there.

One of the beneficial results of the realignment of Poland's frontiers after World War II is the new 430-mile coastline. (Before the war Poland had a coastline of only 85 miles.) Danzig is a thriving shipbuilding center; fishing boats have added almost 200,000 tons of fish yearly to the Polish diet; and the long beach and promenade at Sopot, between Danzig and Gdynia, are crowded with sun worshipers in summer.

THE northern provinces are ideal summer vacation resorts because of the excellent sailing and swimming available in innumerable connecting rivers and lakes. They, too, contain reminders of grimmer times. Just north of the little town of Ketrzyn, in the middle of the Mazurian lakes district, Hitler ordered another redoubt built. This one was a vast affair, with a soaring air-raid watchtower and subterranean chambers many stories below ground level. He called it the Wolf's Lair. It was here in July 1944 that Graf von Stauffenberg, one of the German officers who conspired against Hitler's disastrous leadership at that time, planted the bomb that nearly killed the Führer. Retreating before the Russians later that month, the S.S. blew up the Wolf's Lair. Today it is a concrete shambles covered with moss and dead leaves in a quiet wood.

This area used to be East Prussia, the country of the Teutonic Knights. And there *are* wolves, the nice, nonhuman variety, in the region. Not very far to the southeast of the Wolf's Lair is Białowieża, one of Europe's only virgin forests, a 300-square-mile area that has never been cultivated or grazed and is substantially as it was before history began. Among the protected game is a herd of European bisons; there are also roebucks, deer and boars, for which the visitor can get hunting licenses. In July 1944 Soviet forces came through this forest, took the city of Białystok after a hard fight, outflanked the Wolf's Lair and plunged on toward Warsaw.

That Soviet Army group was but the latest of many attackers of Warsaw in the 600 years since the Dukes of Mazovia set up court on the high western bank of the Vistula on which the city still sits. As long ago as 1408 the settlement, then only the size of a town, was granted a charter and a significant motto: *Contemnit Procellas* (It defies the storm). The storm took shape in the form of the Teutonic Knights, who were defied and defeated at Grunwald, about 80 miles north of Warsaw, in 1410. Warsaw never looked back: the industrious peasants turned the surrounding plains into a granary, and enterprising Poles brought the golden wheat to Warsaw, thence to be shipped down the fast-flowing Vistula to all the ports of northern Europe.

KING SIGISMUND III moved the royal residence from Cracow to Warsaw in 1596. The magnates imported Italian architects and city planners who gave them buildings with classical exteriors like those of Renaissance Italy, but with lavish baroque interiors. The floors were paved with red and black marble; walls were hung with Flemish tapestries; chairs were upholstered in Córdoba leather. The nobles dressed in the style of Rembrandt's *Polish Rider,* and the burghers and rich peasants imitated them. The style was called "Polish baroque," and Poland became "the peacock and the parrot of nations." Alas, Warsaw's treasures became only loot for the Swedish, Saxon, Russian and Prussian armies that marched through the city in the 17th Century.

Yet in 1765 (such is the Polish capacity for recovery) the French encyclopedist Denis Diderot could write: "Warsaw is a beautifully situated town built on the edge of a broad plain rising in terraces above the Vistula. It is ringed with suburbs where the lords have their castles and the monks their monasteries." Some of these castles can still be seen: the Royal Palace in Wilanów, summer abode of King Jan III Sobieski, has been beautifully restored and contains a rich collection of art treasures.

The Warsaw of this period can best be seen and enjoyed in a score of oil paintings by Canaletto, the Venetian, in the National Museum. From the Praga shore the sun falls on a golden sailing barge, with the Royal Palace and city spires in the background; in Miodowa Street a sumptuous coach passes a bonneted nursemaid and an artist displaying his wares on a wall. Life is crowded but leisurely: gallants in tricornered hats ride spirited horses or recline under trees listening to a piper. The 19th Century arrives without industrial shock, and the gallery shows us bluestocking poetesses and romantic young men striking attitudes. A step farther along in the museum and we are in the age of the Nobel laureates: Marie Skłodowska Curie, who discovered radium, and the novelists Henryk Sienkiewicz and Władysław Reymont. The Gallery of Fame does not yet include that later generation, some of whom, like the musicians Artur Rubinstein and Wanda Landowska, went to America; or others of whom, like the novelist Marja Dąbrowska and the poet Antoni Słonimski, stayed home. Theirs was the time, not so long ago, when the streets of Warsaw were full of droshkies, whose drivers wore high boots and long blue coats with license numbers attached to the backs of their collars; when there were always high-style weddings and somber funerals; when toasts were drunk in honey wine laced with vodka.

Old Warsaw died at daybreak on September 1, 1939, when the city was bombed by the Luftwaffe— eight days after the signing of the Hitler-Stalin pact. The First Battle of Warsaw lasted a month. Hospitals were destroyed; the dead were buried in the streets. When the Nazis moved in, museums and galleries were looted, and their treasures were sent to Germany. All universities, colleges and schools were closed.

THE only educational opportunities left to the Poles," said Gauleiter Hans Frank, "should be of a type that will enable them to see the hopelessness of their position." *Die neue deutsche Stadt Warschau* (the new German city of Warsaw) was to be one with a population largely composed of Germans and a labor force of Poles residing in a prison settlement on the opposite bank of the Vistula, according to documents which were produced at Frank's trial at the war-crimes tribunal held in Nuremberg in 1946. The swastika flew over Warsaw; walls were soon covered with posters announcing the death penalty for a multitude of offenses; and every Jewish shop had the Star of David painted on its front.

In the Muranów quarter of Warsaw the Nazis created a mammoth Ghetto. A high brick wall was built around 1,692 buildings, some of which were already war-damaged. The city's Jewish population of 360,000 (later swelled to 500,000 by out-of-town refugees) was herded into this area, which had only two exits. The weekly food ration was systematically cut down until it consisted of a pound of black bread, two ounces of ersatz jam, an ounce of sugar and, occasionally, some potatoes. "We will destroy this tribe," said Gauleiter Ludwig Fischer, the Governor of Warsaw. "They will disappear through hunger and misery." Hunger-crazed children who tried to escape were shot down by guards. A Jewish Council appointed by the Nazis organized living quarters (10 to a room), rationed fuel, set up workshops to make goods to trade for food and maintained religious observances. Typhus and tuberculosis were soon rampant, and every day hundreds of corpses were taken out on wooden carts and buried in the rubble of ruined buildings.

IN 1942 a railroad spur was run into the Ghetto, and carloads of the inhabitants were consigned eastward—to work on farms, they were told, but actually to die in the crematories of Majdanek, Bełzec and a place called Treblinka, a railroad siding on the line to Białystok, about 50 miles from Warsaw. Here the new arrivals were told to take off their clothes for disinfection; the same reason was given for clipping their hair. They were then crushed into large, windowless chambers. In some places steam was turned on, and after an interval the doors were opened and water was hosed on the glued bodies, which were then buried in pits dug by bulldozers. In other places carbon monoxide was piped into the chambers; in still others Cyclon B was used.

The population of the Warsaw Ghetto had been reduced to 70,000 when a Jewish Fighting Organization was formed. Obtaining some weapons and explosives from the underground Polish Home Army, the Jews prepared strong points and caches of food and water inside the Ghetto.

In January 1943 the Jews took their first armed action against the Germans. Under the leadership of Mordechai Anielewicz, a Warsaw student, a group of them attacked an S.S. patrol. The Germans withdrew. A lull followed, but in April Heinrich Himmler, chief of the Gestapo and the S.S., ordered the complete destruction of the Ghetto. On April 19, 1943, the Second Battle of Warsaw began when an S.S. detachment entered the Ghetto under cover of a tank. The tank was attacked with Molotov cocktails and was put out of action. A number of Germans were killed, and the vehicles were burned. A new force of 2,000 S.S. men entered the Ghetto and began burning out every house that offered cover. The battle went on for almost a month, but the Jewish cause was hopeless. On May 8 Mordechai Anielewicz and his last companions, cut off beyond rescue, trapped in a bunker into which the Germans were releasing a suffocating gas, decided upon suicide. Some turned their guns on their companions, others upon themselves; the remainder suffocated. Within days the uprising was over. A handful of Jewish survivors managed to escape through the sewers to join the Polish Home Army.

The Home Army had grown from a small, multi-cell organization to a force of some 300,000 men and women scattered in small groups all over Poland. Most of them were soldiers and officers who wanted to continue the fight against the Nazis; their arms were military weapons taken from Polish arsenals at the time of the 1939 defeat and hidden. Later, with the help of factory workers, they made their own weapons and explosives, including deadly grenades that they called *filipinki*.

AFTER communication between the Home Army and the London Poles had been established, the Home Army became a major source of Allied intelligence about German activities, including the development of the V-1 rocket. The Home Army's main occupation, however, was the sabotage of German transport to and from the Russian front. When the Germans began shooting civilian hostages in reprisal, the Home Army took evidence in secret courts-martial, condemned the guilty German officers to death *in absentia* and notified them when they would be executed.

The cover name of the commander of the Home Army was Bór (forest). Bór was a former colonel in the regular Polish Army whose real name is Tadeusz

Komorowski. General Bór was suspicious of Russian intentions, but when the Nazis began to fall back into Poland before the Russian advance in 1944 he carried out orders from London to contact Soviet forces. Bór sent envoys to the Soviet commanders, but none returned and some were found shot.

T HE fact that both the Poles and the Russians had a common enemy in Nazi Germany was less important to the Soviet Union at this stage of the war than was the control of postwar Poland. The extent of Soviet coolness toward the Home Army became apparent on July 21, 1944, when the Communists set up their Polish Committee of National Liberation at Lublin. As soon as it was established, the committee launched a violent campaign against the Home Army on the radio and in the press.

While General Bór hoped that Stanisław Mikołajczyk, Premier of the London government-in-exile, who had flown to Moscow, would be able to restore diplomatic amity with the Russians, he believed that to stand idle while the Germans retreated and the Russians advanced would be giving the Soviets "the spiteful propaganda argument [of] putting us into the category of silent allies." Bór decided to fight for Warsaw.

Bór's force in Warsaw consisted of 40,000 men and 4,200 women. They could hear the sound of Soviet guns. On July 31 Soviet tanks broke through the German bridgehead on the other side of the Vistula. At exactly 5 o'clock in the afternoon of August 1, 1944, thousands of windows were flung open across the city. "From all sides a hail of bullets struck the passing Germans. In fifteen minutes an entire city of a million inhabitants was engulfed in the fight," Bór recalled in his book *The Secret Army*.

The Poles had a carefully worked-out plan for seizing the strategic points of the city. Despite strong German resistance the plan was successful. The Germans brought in heavy tanks which soon fell victim to Molotov cocktails and *filipinki;* two were captured. In the first week of fighting, Bór's forces occupied nearly half of the city. The Germans reorganized and attacked with flame throwers, heavy mortars and artillery, and air bombardments.

After two weeks of fighting, some support came from British Royal Air Force planes flying 800 miles from Italy—and back again, the Russians having refused them permission to land on the Soviet side of the front. Despite heavy flak (250 Polish and British RAF men were lost), the RAF, coming in low over the smoking city, dropped three million rounds of ammunition and 19,000 grenades, as well as anti-tank guns and small arms. Bór was nevertheless forced out of his headquarters in the factory district west of the demolished Ghetto and set up another in the narrow streets of the Old Town which his men barricaded with paving stones. "We have not eaten any bread for ten days," he radioed. At that point the Soviet Army entered the suburb of Praga, across the river. Bór appealed to Marshal Konstantin Rokossovsky for aid. He received no answer. A desperate hit-and-hide battle took place in the cellars, canals and sewers of the city, with the Germans gradually closing in. On the 43rd day of the struggle Soviet planes finally dropped food and ammunition, and a week later United States Air Corps Flying Fortresses, using Russian bases, parachuted supplies. But on October 2 Bór's men fired their last ammunition, and the next day Bór surrendered. The Third Battle of Warsaw had lasted 63 days, longer than the entire 1939 campaign in Poland and the 1940 campaign in France. Casualties numbered some 250,000 killed or wounded.

L ATER the Russians made explicit their reasons for failing to exploit the bridgehead provided by the Home Army. Arthur Bliss Lane, the American Ambassador to Poland from 1945 to 1947, quotes a member of the Polish Communist Government as remarking: "Had General Bór . . . succeeded in liberating Warsaw [his forces] would have been the heroes of Poland . . . and it would have been most difficult under such circumstances for the Soviet government to maintain in power the Lublin Committee of National Liberation."

After Bór's surrender it took the Soviet Army more than three months to get across the river into Warsaw. Meanwhile the Nazis rounded up 70,000 of the surviving inhabitants of Warsaw and drove them into the countryside. Then came the Sprengkommandos, trained demolition experts who, evidence later showed, had the advice of Nazi architects and art specialists on what required their special attention: the National Museum, for example, depository of the centuries-old municipal and state archives, which they burned. Systematically they went through the city, destroying 16th Century churches, palaces and public buildings, and the statues of the country's great. Thus, in one of his last addresses to the Reichstag, Hitler was able to say: "Warsaw is now no more than a geographical term on the map of Europe." When the Soviet Army finally did enter the city it found, according to its own survey, 25,000 graves in the city streets and 100,000 mines and unexploded missiles in the ruins. Only 15 per cent of the buildings were in any way serviceable, and there was no water, electricity or gas supply.

But people poured back into Warsaw. By the end of the war, there were as many as 400,000 people living in the windowless shells of houses, in cellars and in shanties. Some 20 million cubic yards of rubble had to be removed, and power conduits, water pipes and sewers had to be reinstalled. The Old Town, a small area within the modern city of Warsaw, was rebuilt on its former foundations (it had already been reconstructed once, after World War I). To build it again, fragments of Gothic portals and stained glass discovered in the rubble were used. Cobblestones were relaid, and iron grilles were replaced. Today the Old Town looks as if no shot had ever been fired in its vicinity.

The statue of King Sigismund was put back together and replaced on its tall column. St. Anne's Church, which had been a flame-licked shell, is complete with Gothic apse and a new interior, although St. John's Cathedral can make no pretense to being more than a fresh brick reconstruction of its old 14th Century self. Along Cracow Avenue the German demolition squads were, happily, often defeated by the sheer weight of 19th Century masonry. By patching and straightening, the Reconstruction Office has been able to present fair representations of the building where Marie Curie worked on X-rays and of

PROUD MERMAID is Warsaw's emblem. In legend she met a prince and then a fisherman named Wars and his wife Szawa at the site of modern-day Warsaw. She directed the prince to found a city there.

the Radziwiłł Palace, now the seat of the Council of Ministers. Sheer ponderousness saved the Carmelite church, but one can only conjecture how the Church of the Holy Cross managed to preserve the urn containing Chopin's heart.

And then one enters Nowy Swiat which is again, as before, a street of shops leading to the legation district, where the new U.S. Embassy stands firm and brilliant, like a Fifth Avenue bank; farther down the hill is the Soviet Embassy. Destroyers of cities seldom pause to remember the parks and gardens; thus the Ujazdowski and Lazienki Parks, and the palaces which they surround, are exactly as they were when Canaletto painted them so long ago. Here on summer evenings the Varsovians come to breathe the air of memories past.

If the life of a nation is characterized by its constructions, then the life of modern Warsaw is different indeed from that of old Warsaw. For while the Old Town was being restored, a new, expanding city of institutions and housing developments, broad boulevards and vast, cement-paved squares was spreading over the ruins of the rest of the city, including the conveniently atomized rubble of the former Ghetto. Of the great frowning blocks of new Warsaw, where the headquarters of the Communist Party, the Government offices and the law courts are situated, it can only be said that their architecture is in the modern penitentiary style.

If the Poles did not understand in 1944 how much of a prison their country was to become under Soviet rule, they were soon enlightened by the banning of foreign newspapers and the jamming of foreign broadcasts, the rejection of Marshall Plan aid, the ceaseless flow of abuse of the Vatican and the United States, the arbitrary arrests and rigged trials. Thousands of Polish priests, including then-Archbishop Stefan Wyszyński, and Home Army soldiers were imprisoned. So, too, were members of the Polish Communist Party who were suspected of nationalist deviations. If there were any doubts about who owned the prison, the Poles had only to glance at the proconsul-like posture of Marshal Rokossovsky, commander of the Soviet forces in Poland, and it was not necessary to look very hard to detect the presence of a whole panel of Soviet secret police operators. The barbed-wire barriers encircled the whole country.

ONE of the few old buildings still intact in the vicinity of Warsaw at the end of the war was the Natolin Palace. It became the country residence of Soviet Ambassador Panteleimon Ponomarenko. Here, in 1956, the pro-Russian Polish Communists who favored the continuance of Stalinist methods after the death of Stalin plotted to control the wave of antiparty agitation which swept through Poland that year following an uprising in the city of Poznań, where the wages of workers in the ZISPO engineering works had been cut back and production norms had been increased. Attempts by the workers' union to improve conditions through meetings with local Communist Party officials and by appeals to Warsaw failed; a strike was called in June. The workers had planned a peaceful march to the center of the city to dramatize their demands, but when the march began other citizens joined in; signs demanding "bread and freedom" were displayed; cries against the Russians and the secret police were raised. When the crowd became violent Soviet troops and members of the police opened fire. Hundreds of people fell; the regime later stated that the losses amounted to 53 dead and 300 wounded.

The thaw in the Soviet Union after Stalin's death had had its cautious counterpart in Poland. Some 30,000 political prisoners had been granted amnesty; the Communist poet Adam Ważyk had written "Poem for Adults," asking for "a clear truth . . . the bread of freedom." But denunciation of the "cult of personality"—the phrase used in the Communist world to denote adulation for Stalin and all his works —had not yet led to sweeping changes in Poland. Although the Russians were bent on some administrative changes inside Russia, they had no intention of abandoning their satellite empire. In July 1956 the Central Committee of the Polish Communist Party held a meeting to which Marshal Nikolai Bulganin, who then shared power in the Soviet Union with Nikita Khrushchev, was refused admittance. Although the committee members agreed to rehabilitate Władysław Gomułka, the leader who had been expelled from the party in 1949 on charges of Titoism, it was obvious that a serious rift was developing between the pro-Russian Polish Communists and a more liberal group that favored extensive revision of the party and the administration. Led by Gomułka and First Secretary Edward Ochab, the revisionist cause gained strength when party abuses and secret police brutality were exposed during open trials of the Poznań workers.

The pro-Russians were, however, by no means defeated. A few days before a Central Committee meeting on October 19, they drew up an arrest list of revisionists with 700 names on it. At the same time there were reports that Soviet troops were moving toward Warsaw; Soviet naval vessels demonstrated in the Bay of Danzig. The revisionists countered by instructing General Wacław Komar, head of the Internal Security Corps—the only Polish military body outside the command of Marshal Rokossovsky—to deploy his troops at strategic points around Warsaw. Thousands of students and workers were organized and armed. Eventually word of the impending arrests reached Komar. He tightened security measures to protect the threatened men.

AS the Central Committee meeting got under way Khrushchev himself, fearful that the revisionists would prevail, arrived in Warsaw with several of his top aides to attend the meeting. Ochab suspended the session and with Gomułka and several of their supporters took the Russians to the Belvedere Palace. There they forcefully argued their case, making the point that excessive Soviet interference in Polish internal affairs was destroying the efficiency of the system; the key phrase became "the Polish road to Socialism." While Soviet and Polish troops warily watched each other not far from Warsaw, Khrushchev blustered angrily about "counterrevolutionary activity" and "danger to the whole Socialist camp." But after almost 24 hours of uninterrupted talk Khrushchev bought the argument, called off his assassins and returned home. The victory made a national hero of Gomułka, especially when he arranged for the return of Marshal Rokossovsky and the bulk of his troops to Russia. For years afterward Gomułka and Khrushchev kissed each other on both cheeks when they met.

Varsovians breathed deeply of their new freedoms in 1957. The straitjacket of "socialist realism"—insistence by the Soviet overlords upon the grandiose pictorialization of Communist heroes and achievements—was cast off. Painters burst into Cubism, Surrealism and Abstractionism; youth went wild about jazz; the works of very modern composers were played in the academies. For the first time since the war, writers wrote honestly about life, and a new school of film directors received critical acclaim abroad. Polish professors went visiting in the West, and distinguished self-exiles returned home. The imprisoned priests were released. Wyszyński, a cardinal by this time, traveled to Rome, where he told a fellow prelate whose half-empty church he had attended that "in my Poland there is not enough room in the churches for the faithful." Poland became the only Communist country where priests walked the streets wearing the long robe called the soutane.

A SECTION of privately owned shops selling small goods appeared in the center of the capital. Workers went to the factories secure in the knowledge that henceforth union officials would be elected by secret ballot. Thousands of Stalinists were fired from bureaucratic jobs.

But gradually the luster of freedom faded. Gomułka tried at first to steer a middle-of-the-road course, attempting simultaneously to keep the Russians quiescent and to meet the demands for still more freedom from Polish intellectuals. But, trapped by Poland's economic dependence upon Russia and the Soviet bloc as a whole, Gomułka found that he could not meet the demands of both sides. He brought out the old, stale Communist slogans, took action against critical newspapers and reintroduced censorship. The liberal Ministers of Culture and Education were replaced, and pro-Stalinists were brought back into the party leadership. A general crackdown began. Petty harassments were launched against the Roman Catholic Church.

In the early 1960s, there were recurrent shortages of food and essential goods. Household shopping became an all-day occupation and the expression "nie ma" (there is none) an ironical joke. Hit by discriminatory taxes, the private shops were forced to sell Italian shoes and French sweaters at three times the prices for which they were being sold in their countries of origin. Wages had never been high in Poland: a monthly 1,900 zloty for a worker, 2,500 zloty for a qualified engineer. Who then could afford the state-produced Warszawa car at 100,000 zloty, or even the Syrena at 80,000? A popular crack was: "Our plan goes so well, it's as bad now as it would be in two years." With 25 million gallons of alcoholic beverages being consumed every year, alcoholism was becoming a national problem, and drunken driving was becoming one of the city's chief hazards. City "drying-out" stations were crowded; 313,000 people were picked up for drunkenness in 1962.

In the gay cellars like the Amigo the attraction is not the food or the drink, but the hubbub of talk; sharp at 10 p.m. the band stops, the waiters withdraw, and the clientele is ushered out into the vast, dimly lighted territory which is Warsaw at night. Security police measures have been stepped up; Poles in regular contact with Western foreigners are obliged to explain the relationship. The visitor can *feel* that his hotel room is bugged. Behind the back of his hand the waiter says, "It is not as bad as it was in Stalin's time, when children had to inform on their parents, but it is still bad."

TODAY Poland seems tired; it is not the Poland of a few years ago. What has happened since the glorious days of 1956? Certainly the economy is out of joint, but to say that is merely to give a partial answer to a profoundly complex question. Perhaps more of the answer can be seen by glimpsing the Palace of Culture and Science, a skyscraper the Russians built at the center of Warsaw. It rises 30 floors and is topped by 300 feet of glittering spike. Looking like a scaled-down copy of Moscow University, the palace symbolizes an alien culture. Discontent simmers on all levels throughout Poland, and while the country can look inward to ancient traditions and recent glories and quietly enlarge contacts and contracts with the West, it can never ignore the Soviet shadow to the east.

The Endless Trials of the Poles

Yesterday and today tragedy has haunted Poland. Since the mid-17th Century the country has been invaded, devastated and partitioned by its rapacious neighbors. Yet the Poles have always retained a fanatic devotion to freedom. Independence was obtained at the end of World War I—and swiftly rendered meaningless by harsh domestic regimes. During World War II Poland was a center of conflict; almost one fifth of its people died; millions were deported for slave labor in Germany. Although the Soviet Union still casts a watchful eye on the land, the people have their Church, their own farms and a relatively liberal Communist Government.

COMMUNIST LEADERS, Władysław Gomułka (*above, at right*), Party Secretary in Poland, and Anastas Mikoyan, a top Soviet official, chat at a reception in Warsaw.

EARNEST DIPLOMATS exchange views at the reception. Poland has some domestic independence, but its foreign-affairs position parallels that of the Russians.

SOMBER CROWD in front of a statue symbolizing resistance to the Nazis (*opposite*) watches the funeral procession of Aleksander Zawadzki, President until 1964.

MOUNDS OF RUBBLE, grim reminders of the destruction of the Warsaw Ghetto by the Nazis in 1943, remain in view of modern buildings. Some 50,000 Jews died in a final, hopeless, month-long defense of the Ghetto.

GUTTED BUILDINGS of Elblag, bombed by Allied aircraft when it was a part of Germany, have never been torn down *(right)*. Warsaw suffered even more: street fighting and bombing ravaged 87 per cent of the city.

the cities of Poland still carry terrible scars testifying to the savagery of the conflict

A SIMPLER ERA survives in the pastoral Tatra mountain region of the south

MODEST CHURCH, built in 1757, stands in Obidowa in southern Poland *(opposite)*. Many such structures still exist, recalling the centuries when Polish villages were built entirely of wood.

GRAZING SHEEP move slowly across a pasture as two shepherds urge them along on a quiet afternoon. The sheep are privately owned, as are most of the farms and livestock in Poland.

TIRED SHEPHERDS wait for supper in their hut. Shepherds in this area still carry traditional axlike crooks and wear the ancient costume of white felt trousers, broad belts and black hats.

*URBAN LIVING requires hard work
from most families but offers
cultural advantages and modern stores*

YOUNG WIFE, Mrs. Henryka Mordelski stands in front of the new apartment building in a Warsaw suburb where she, her husband and their small son live. She has a well-paying job as a typesetter in a printing plant.

NURSERY CHILD, Marek Mordelski *(opposite)* snacks on cake and tea at a state-run child-care center. The family is rarely together, since the parents work on different shifts. Marek spends seven hours a day in the nursery.

THE MORDELSKIS gather around the dining table in their small apartment, part of a development for young couples. The parents sleep and eat in this room, and Marek has his own room. Jan Mordelski is a foreman in

HUGE BOOKSTORE in Warsaw offers works by writers from most of the world's nations. Although an impressive number of books are published in Poland, the state suppresses some by claiming a "paper shortage."

an electrical plant. With their combined incomes—and by staying at their jobs during vacations—the couple has been able to buy a television set on the install-ment plan. They also own a Czechoslovak motorcycle.

BUSY SUPERMARKET in Warsaw uses U.S. self-service selling techniques. Food costs in Poland have increased by a full 17 per cent since 1958. While meat is occasion-ally hard to obtain, there is no general food shortage.

7

Prague the Enduring

"KINGLY Prague! Indescribable, incomparable is the splendor of thy churches, the beauty of thy palaces," wrote the German novelist Friedrich de la Motte-Fouqué in 1823. People have been making ecstatic remarks about Prague ever since the legendary medieval Princess Libuše looked down on this bend of the river Vltava and exclaimed: "I see a city whose glory shall reach the stars." Pope Pius II found Prague the equal of Florence; the French sculptor Auguste Rodin called it "the Northern Rome." Today one may feel differently, not because a layer of industrial soot covers the ancient stone, or because the splendid churches are for the most part deserted and the beautiful palaces changed into

state museums or offices, or even because Prague's historic thoroughfares are crowded with rattletrap red trams and unsmiling people. What strikes one about Prague today is the function of architecture as an expression of changing political fortune.

The city's humble beginnings were in primitive wooden forts on both sides of the river. The wooden buildings vanished in the hearths of that militant Christianity which expressed its aspirations toward, and its belief in, eternity by erecting its buildings in enduring stone. Among buildings remaining from that epoch, in the style called Romanesque, are the Rotunda of the Holy Rood in the section known as the Old Town, the Basilica of St. George and the

Black Tower in the Prague Castle complex on Hradčany Hill.

Romanesque Prague was built over by succeeding dynasties or political systems which sought to assert their own permanence in stone and utilized specific architectural styles to do so—Gothic, Renaissance, baroque, Neo-Gothic, Bauhaus, Stalinist.

The pointed arches and flying buttresses of Gothic, that most soaring of styles, were brought to Prague in the 14th Century—and Gothic suggests better than words can describe the historic ascendancy of Christianity over Slav paganism, and of the Germans over the Czechs. Gothic constructions —the Old Town Bridge Tower, the Charles Bridge over the Vltava and the twin spires of the Týn Church— convey an unsurpassed serenity. On the other hand St. Vitus' Cathedral on Hradčany Hill barely reconciles a triumphant sense of temporal power with the spiritual. It is a royal church, in which Bohemian kings were crowned before the high altar.

Gothic can, however, also be humble and popular. The Old Town Hall, the meeting place centuries ago of the Bohemian Diet and of assemblies of the followers of the 14th Century Bohemian nationalist and religious reformer John Hus, is, so to speak, people's Gothic. Visitors still come from afar to watch the long, gilded hands of the astronomical clock on the Old Town Hall's eastern wall move toward a specified hour when a cock crows and a door flies open. A procession of iron figures representing the Twelve Apostles jerkily emerges and then returns within. The clock was made in 1490 by Master Hanuš of Růže. According to legend his eyes were put out for fear he would make another like it; as the old clockmaster was dying, the tradition says, he put his hand into the works and the clock stopped for centuries.

A story no less macabre is told about the final struggle for Prague at the end of World War II. The U.S. Third Army reached Pilsen, only 55 miles away,

in May 1945. General Dwight Eisenhower suggested to the Soviet Chief of Staff, General Aleksei Antonov, that the Americans should liberate Prague. Antonov, whose armies were still tied down to the east by German forces, coldly rejected the idea. But the citizens of Prague, anticipating the arrival of the Americans, rose against the Germans. When the Americans failed to appear, the Germans shot hundreds of Praguers. Master Hanuš' clock stopped once again in the middle of the fighting.

Even the city's Old-New Synagogue, the oldest surviving Jewish house of worship in Eastern Europe, is Gothic. Originally constructed about 1270, it was rebuilt in 1536 with typical Gothic arches and vault.

At that time the Jewish community lived under severe restrictions which were not to be fully lifted until the 19th Century. The limitations of the medieval Ghetto are indicated by the Old Jewish Cemetery. Because the Jews were not permitted to enlarge it, the dead were buried in layers, and the tombstones and sarcophagi are packed closely together. The last burial was in 1787. By then an estimated 200,000 persons had been interred in the cemetery. Before the arrival of the Nazis, there were some 35,000 Jews in Prague; it is not known how many there are in the city today, but 10,000 is an informed guess. Only a steadfast minority, mostly older people, attends the Old-New Synagogue today.

One of the most imposing tombstones in the cemetery is that of Rabbi Yehuda Löw, who died in 1609. A story is told that the rabbi used to bring a figure fashioned of clay to life by placing in its mouth a parchment bearing a magic inscription. Such a clay man was known as a golem in medieval Jewish legends. The golem worked tirelessly for the rabbi, except on the Sabbath, when the rabbi would take the parchment from its mouth and the golem would become clay again. One Sabbath eve the rabbi forgot to take out the parchment and the golem ran amuck, terrifying people and

---

CZECHOSLOVAKIA: BASIC FACTS

AREA: 49,359 square miles

POPULATION: 13,970,000

MONETARY UNIT: The koruna (valued at about $.14 at the official exchange rate, about $.07 at the more realistic tourist rate). This book employs the official rate except when noted.

MAJOR EXPORTS: Machinery, fuels, minerals, metals, consumer goods

RELIGIONS: Roman Catholic, Protestant, Czechoslovak Church, Orthodox

---

destroying everything in its path until the courageous rabbi took the parchment from its mouth and the golem again became clay. This time the rabbi let the golem remain so.

The legend runs deep down into Czech life and may have been one of the inspirations for Karel Capek's play *Rossum's Universal Robots (R.U.R.)*, which was a New York stage success in 1922. In it the near-human robots revolt against man's domination and take over the world. A new word was introduced into the English language (from the Czech word *"robota,"* or "forced labor") and a new idea: that man might eventually be destroyed by forcing other beings to do his own tasks. Capek wrote about the conflict between dictatorship and democracy in another play called *The White Sickness*. A profound believer in Czech democracy, Capek died soon after the Munich agreement of 1938.

NOT far from the Old Jewish Cemetery is the little Gothic church called St. Martin's-in-the-Wall, which was literally built into the city wall in the 12th Century. Here, in the 15th Century, John Hus's follower Master Jakoubek of Stříbro dispensed Communion "in both kinds," that is, with wine as well as bread—a practice reserved in Roman Catholic ritual for the clergy alone. This ceremony gave the Hussite movement its popular symbol: a chalice. It was a Gothic window of the New Town City Hall from which the New Town councilors were thrown in 1419—one of the acts of violence which led up to the Hussite wars—although the building pointed out to the visitor in Charles Square today has undergone several transformations since then.

Two centuries later, when Count Heinrich Matthias von Thurn, protesting against the closing and razing of Protestant churches in Bohemia, cried, "Out of the window with them," it was certainly a Gothic window from which two of the Emperor's governors fell (harmlessly onto refuse in the moat, according to some, who see God's prejudice in the affair). This celebrated defenestration, however, may have been the last historic act in which the Gothic style predominated; the religious wars which then began were followed by the baroque.

The baroque style developed in the late 16th Century after the Roman Catholic Church had been revitalized by the Council of Trent, which redefined Catholic objectives and practices in reaction to the Protestant Reformation. Inspired by Pope Sixtus V's injunction that Rome needed not only sacred and spiritual power, "but also beauty which ensures convenience and worldly ornamentation," the Church found the new style eminently suitable. Baroque is an expansive style, employing motifs borrowed from the late Roman era, with ornate embellishments. It was designed to evoke popular admiration and at the same time to express, by sheer richness, an indestructible temporal and spiritual power.

The Jesuits came to Prague in 1556 and built the Clementinum, their college, in the new style. After the Prague Castle the Clementinum remains the largest building complex in the city. The old Church of St. Salvator was rebuilt as the Clementinum's chapel in the new image. Its two-story façade is ornamented with Corinthian pilasters; inside, the nave is set about with chapels and polished marble statuary. The walls are ornamented with gold leaf. General Albrecht Wallenstein, Duke of Friedland, a Czech nobleman who had distinguished himself in the service of the Holy Roman Emperor during the Thirty Years' War, razed a whole area near the Prague Castle and built himself one of the finest palaces of the baroque age. Soon Prague glistened with façades and towers of richly curving stone.

THE success of the Counter Reformation is nowhere better symbolized than in the Church of St. Nicholas, one of the most beautiful churches in Europe. Built in the Lesser Town between 1703 and 1753—a period in which Bohemian baroque reached its height—the church is impressive in size alone. The curved front and ribbed dome give an impression of strength; the interior is sumptuous and graceful, with deep, ornate chapels and graceful statuary. Talented Czech and Austrian artists and architects were already subtly changing the Italian master design. Before many years passed, the onion spire became an important local variant. Statues and paintings by Bohemian artists of St. Wenceslas and St. Ludmilla and other locally revered saints have a freshness and appeal which distinguish them from the works of the Italian masters of the same period. The style spread through the land. Perhaps the most characteristic feature of the Bohemian landscape is the constantly repeated sight of baroque saints on watch at crossroads; of St. John of Nepomuk, protector against floods, guarding bridges everywhere; of paintings and statues of St. Florian, eternally on the alert against the possibility of houses' being struck by lightning.

At the end of the 18th Century, when the romantic movement began to spread through Europe, poets, artists and novelists became absorbed in the past. Medieval Gothic architecture was rediscovered; architects began to use Gothic motifs. This Neo-Gothic style can be said to be an expression of the reaction of the 18th and 19th Centuries against rationalism and classicism.

Both medieval Gothic and Neo-Gothic survive in modern Prague, and the two styles are frequently mixed. The Powder Tower, a genuine piece of medieval Gothic, has been decorated, for example, with crests and blazons which are Neo-Gothic; the twin spires of the Church of Sts. Peter and Paul have small Neo-Gothic curlicues. St. Vitus' Cathedral is a Gothic masterpiece dating from the 14th Century, although portions of it are later additions; some were built as late as 1929.

IN the baroque era, opera had come to the Czech lands. An art form at first restricted to the court and to noblemen's homes, it soon found acceptance among the people. The Czechs long had found solace from their hatred of serfdom, of military service and of German overlordship in songs of love and nature. Czech music later turned to instrumentation and to the development of the sonata form. These developments prepared the way for the success in Prague of the music of the Austrian composer Wolfgang Amadeus Mozart. To Mozart, kingly Prague was a home. He often stayed with his friend the Czech composer František Jan Dušek at the Villa Bertramka, which is now a museum containing Mozart memorabilia. Mozart's opera *Don Giovanni* was given its première in Prague. The story is told that he had forgotten to compose the overture and was reminded to do so at the last moment by Dušek's wife. The music sheets for the overture were brought to the orchestra just as the curtain was about to rise, and as the opening bars were played the audience

burst into loud applause. *"Meine Prager verstehen mich"* (My Praguers understand me), Mozart is reported to have said.

In 1796 Ludwig van Beethoven lodged at the Golden Unicorn, a hotel on Bath Street; Franz Liszt, Richard Wagner and Hector Berlioz gave concerts in the Neo-Renaissance building on Slavonic Island, close to the right bank of the river. For three years Antonín Dvořák was organist at the Church of St. Adalbert.

NOT surprisingly, there was a great deal of architectural change in Prague when the Republic of Czechoslovakia was established after World War I. The Roman Catholic Church had been closely linked with the Habsburg Empire, and 1.4 million Czechs renounced Roman Catholicism. Many of them joined the new National Church. The crucifix was removed from schools, and a brief wave of iconoclasm swept Prague: statues of the Habsburgs suffered, as well as monuments erected by the Jesuits, and there was a moment when St. John of Nepomuk was in danger of being toppled from the Charles Bridge into the Vltava. The wave of anti-Catholicism soon subsided, but as late as 1924 the papal nuncio quit town in protest against Government participation in the Hus anniversary celebrations. The black flag of the Hussites, bearing the symbolic red chalice, had been flown from the presidential palace.

The republic's preferred architectural style was a variation of Bauhaus, after the name of a then revolutionary school of German architects. Nevertheless, the brief career of the republic may be said to have ended on a baroque note. For it was from the Cernín Palace, the largest baroque building in Prague and then, as now, the Foreign Office, that Jan Masaryk fell or was pushed to his death in 1948. Fell? In Prague some believe that he was murdered by the STB, the Communist secret police. No one can know for certain; there was no autopsy, and no friend was allowed to approach the scene or to examine the body before burial.

In the street named Na bojišti (On the Battlefield), there is a tavern called At the Sign of the Chalice. This is the inn to which that engaging character of Czech fiction created by Jaroslav Hašek, Good Soldier Schweik, came regularly for his beer until that unhappy day when he fell into conversation with a police agent and was arrested for political unreliability. It was also at this tavern that Schweik promised to meet his pal Vodička after service in the Austrian Army during World War I. Schweik's technique of fighting Austrian bureaucracy by playing the role of a willing but stupidly naïve fellow is said to epitomize the Czechs' passive resistance under the Austrian yoke. For a time in the 1950s, as the Communist grip on the country tightened, gay little models of the Good Soldier Schweik turned up in Czech homes; it was not resistance to Austrian oppression that was symbolized by the Good Soldier.

The racks of European newspapers which used to be found in Prague cafés have disappeared today and with them much of the vibrant intellectual and political life of the country. Instead, the newspapers are full of such phrases as "correct orientation" and "political criminals" and the cynical use of old Hussite expressions about "the people." There are confectionery shops with elaborate and expensive pastries, and the *horky parky* (hot dog) vendors still cry their wares. Shops are full of expensive but often shoddy merchandise and inferior dress fabrics. In the Klement Gottwald Museum, under a glass case, is to be found a gilt-edged edition of the works of Walter Ulbricht, the East German party leader who was the architect of the Berlin Wall.

On the map Czechoslovakia looks like a sponge that is being squeezed from all sides. Politics and history gave the country its shape; its crosshatch of mountain systems was created by quarreling geologic upheavals. As a result the country lies at the European triple divide, the source of rivers flowing into the North Sea, the Black Sea and the Baltic. The Czechs live in Bohemia and Moravia-Silesia. Bohemia is boxed in by the hill country of the Bohemian Forest in the southwest and by the Ore Mountains in the northeast. Through the Moravian Depression, which divides the country from the

DEFIANT LIONS surround Prague's old crest. In 1964 the city replaced the upper lion's crown—symbol of the Habsburg monarchy—with a star and substituted a flame for the cross on the top shield. The legend reads: "Prague, mother of cities."

northeast to the southwest, streams flow south to the Danube and north to the Baltic. The Slovaks live amid the mountains to the east. The country has been inhabited for millennia; Upper Paleolithic excavations near Brno have brought to light human hearths believed to date from 20,000 B.C. The Celts who lived here called themselves the Boii, from which the Romans got Boiohaemia, hence Bohemia.

Czechoslovakia is a heavily forested country, one third of its area being covered by firs, spruces, oaks, beeches and junipers. The great national park in the High Tatra is wild; here are found orchids, balsams, dog's-tooth violets and gentians. In the years since the old hunting estates were nationalized, wildlife has increased, and there are many more deer today than there were a century ago. In the Giant Mountains are grouse; in the High Tatra are chamois, marmots and bears, all known and numbered. The steady drift of people to the cities and the expulsion of the Germans give the countryside a sparse, empty appearance, but the raising of sugar beets and potatoes, wheat, oats, rye and barley—the source of the famous Bohemian malt—goes on very much as it has for centuries. At Zatec in the late summer the air is thick with the rich, inebriating odor of hundreds of acres of hops ripening in the sun.

The country contains nearly a hundred castles worth inspection by visitors. Some are romantic hilltop ruins or frowning fortresses built to dominate rivers and valleys. Others were well-appointed residences. One of these is the Castle of Litomyšl, which contains a charming theater with backdrops De Chirico might have painted. Another is the Wallenstein Castle at Mnichovo Hradiště, which has a rich collection of porcelain and a library of 22,000 volumes and many medieval manuscripts. Legends still cling to some castles, as to that of Cachtice in Slovakia, where, in the 16th Century, a cruel Countess Bathory is said to have tried to recapture her fading looks by bathing in the blood of young girls. At

121

some castle gates the tourist is waved on; using castles as prisons is not a new practice in Czechoslovakia. The fortress of Terezín, a gloomy edifice on the Elbe about 40 miles north of Prague, long used as a regular penitentiary, became a political prison when the Nazis took over Czechoslovakia. The town of Terezín became a ghetto and collection center from which 86,934 Jews were sent on to their deaths in Polish gas chambers.

THERE are towns or groups of towns designated as historical art preserves. The country is rich in religious shrines, the most important being that of Our Lady of the Svatá Hora, a hill above Příbram. Thousands of pilgrims journey to it each year. The birthplace of John Hus is at Husinec, and at Tábor are the remains of fortifications built by Jan Žižka, the warrior-defender of the Hussites. For students of history, there is the battlefield of Austerlitz, near Brno, where Napoleon defeated the Austrian and Russian Armies in 1805; its grassy expanse is now spotted with appropriate plaques. And near Hradec Králové in East Bohemia, at the scene of the decisive Battle of Sadowa in the 1866 Prusso-Austrian war, there is a high lookout from which the movements of the various regiments can be traced.

Not quite a battlefield is a street crossing in Prague where, in May 1942, Czech parachutists who had been dropped from British planes ambushed and fatally wounded Reinhard Heydrich, the Nazi "Protector" of Bohemia-Moravia. In retribution Hitler ordered the nearby village of Lidice "wiped from the face of the earth." All the men in the village were killed, the women taken to concentration camps and the children shipped off to educational institutions. The village itself was broken up stone by stone, stick by stick. Ashes and sand were smoothed over. Today the site is a rose garden, a pause on the tourist route to more tangible scars of history. Nearby a new Lidice of modern housing units has grown up.

Volcanoes which were once active in the region left Czechoslovakia the hot springs at the towns of Karlsbad, Marienbad and Franzensbad, where the princes and potentates of Europe once came to plunge and plot. There are hundreds of other mineral springs with medicinal properties. The hot, sulphurous mud to be found at Piešt'any on the river Váh is said to be singularly effective in cases of arthritis. Caves, underground lakes and cataracts honeycomb the limestone regions, and at Dobšiná in Slovakia, there is a cavern where uncounted tons of ice form a frozen waterfall that never thaws and a cavern floor on which one can ice skate at any time. Near Brno there is an abyss that is "measureless to man." Not least among Czechoslovakia's natural wonders are the crystal-clear spring waters from which are made the justly famous Pilsner and Budweiser beers.

Bohemian glass and porcelain are made from the fine silica sand, kaolin and clay deposits in the northwest. In the 13th Century, gold mined at Jílové was made into ducats stamped with an owl, while the minting of coins from the silver of Kutná Hora did so much for the local economy that the mine owners erected the magnificent church of St. Barbara, patron saint of mining, as a mark of gratitude. Iron and bituminous coal in close proximity were the foundation of the famous Skoda armament works. Hard coal mined at Ostrava feeds the furnaces which forge iron ore from Slovakia and the Ukraine. Ores extracted from mines at Příbram and elsewhere in the country make Czechoslovakia a major supplier of uranium to the Soviet Union.

EXCEPT for the foehn, a warm breeze which thaws snow in springtime, Czechoslovakia is not a country of high winds: dark, vaporous coal smoke lies heavy over many a shining valley. It is an industrial country, about the size of New York State, that once had a living standard comparable to those of Austria and Germany. Its highly diversified heavy and light industries and rich agricultural land produced export goods and plentiful food and clothing for its citizens, and made advanced social services possible. But less than two decades of Communist rule and Russian overlordship have run down the economy, killed enthusiasm, and made life drab and regimented. There is apathy among the old, but there is a new wave of questioning by the young, and the questions become increasingly insistent. A new generation of Czechoslovakians is demanding new ethics, new decency in high places and a new humanism—one, perhaps, that will match the traditions of kingly Prague.

Dispossessed owners, members of the Wratislaw family live in a cottage on the grounds of their former estate in southern Bohemia.

The Continuing Hardships of a Young Nation

Czechoslovakia, a country which came into existence as a national entity less than 50 years ago, has experienced more than its share of disaster. In 1938 Czechoslovakia was handed over to Nazi Germany in a vain effort to appease Hitler's ambitions. The country felt the full weight of Nazi occupation during World War II; after the war it enjoyed a brief period of democratic freedom, then found itself once more under totalitarianism: in 1948 the Communists obtained control of the Government and plunged the nation into police-state "Stalinism." The planners took over; the dynamic factories which Hitler had coveted, and which had made the country into one of Europe's most industrialized nations, were forced to overproduce. Resources were squandered, the quality of goods deteriorated, and the cost of living soared. Today, although economic controls are relaxing somewhat, and the standard of living remains a cut above those of its Eastern European neighbors, the Czechoslovaks face continuing difficulties.

ENDURING STRUCTURES of
ancient towns and once-great estates
lend the countryside an air of grandeur

RENAISSANCE CASTLE in Bohemia is mirrored in a pond. Czechoslovakia has more than 2,000 castles, most of which are now state-owned schools, hospitals or recreation centers.

GRACEFUL CHERUB stands in the town square of Telč *(opposite)*. The statue was added after the historic square—with its simple Renaissance houses and long arcades—was constructed.

TOWN SQUARE is a gathering place for citizens of Tábor, in central Bohemia. A center of the rebellious 15th Century Hussite movement, Tábor is now a bustling town of 18,000 people.

VENERABLE CAPITAL, Prague remains one of the loveliest cities in the world

IRREGULAR HOUSES are packed together along the narrow streets of the Lesser Town of Prague. In the background, the Vltava River winds through the center of the city. While Prague suffered relatively minor air-raid damage during World War II and most of its handsome old buildings are intact, the streets are dirty and many of the houses are in a state of decay.

STONE BRIDGE spanning the Vltava in Prague is bathed in violet hues at sunset as boaters drift slowly under its arches. When it was constructed in the 14th Century this bridge was the only approach to Prague Castle, and consequently was strongly fortified. "Prague of the Hundred Towers" is renowned for its architecture, especially its many delicate church spires.

YOUNG MARRIED COUPLE, Frank and Jana Madl sit in their small apartment in Prague. They are relatively successful members of the proletariat. He is a machinist, she a hairdresser.

DILIGENT EMPLOYEE, Frank Madl works in the machine-tool factory where he has been employed since 1954. Like his father before him, Madl is a member of the Communist Party.

A MEASURE OF AFFLUENCE is available to Praguers whose skills are in demand by state

ON THEIR MOTOR SCOOTER, a prized possession, the Madls ride through city traffic. Jana earns a salary of about $150 a month, roughly half what Frank makes as a skilled laborer.

BALLET ADMIRERS, the Madls watch a performance of *Swan Lake (left).* Because the price of theater tickets is so low, they are able to attend a play, opera or ballet at least once a week.

IN A CLASSROOM at the Prague Technical College a professor draws a diagram in an electrical-theory course. The country has no particular shortage of engineers, but lacks skilled labor.

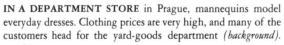

IN A DEPARTMENT STORE in Prague, mannequins model everyday dresses. Clothing prices are very high, and many of the customers head for the yard-goods department *(background)*.

IN A SUBURB of Bratislava, a major center of industry in Slovakia, a teacher takes her young class on an outing past new high-rise apartment buildings and recently erected power lines.

An increasing flow of country people into the cities has created a severe housing shortage: there are more persons per room in Czechoslovakia than in most other European nations.

In a vain effort to bring down a Russian observation plane, Hungarian street fighters fire rifles into the sky on November 3, 1956, the day

before Soviet tanks moved into Budapest to put down the rebellion.

Budapest the Brave

EAST of Vienna the river Danube forms the north-west border of Hungary for almost a hundred miles. It then enters the Visegrád Gorge and makes the "Danube bend" southward, bisecting the whole of Hungary at the 19th degree of longitude. It is a historic division. The Romans used the great, deep-flowing river as a natural bulwark against the barbarians. The land to the south and west of the river formed the Roman province of Pannonia, or Transdanubia as it is still called.

Clusters of irregularly spaced mountain ranges stretch across Transdanubia, some of the mountaintops bearing the ruins of ancient forts. Beech and oak forests clothe their slopes, and the valleys between them are a patchwork of green and brown fields watered by the innumerable tributaries of the Danube and other rivers. The crops are mostly corn, wheat, barley and rye, laced in summer with poppies and sunflowers. Orchards and vineyards as well flourish in the porous soil.

Some of the valleys are bustling with industrial life. There are manganese deposits, bauxite mines and aluminum foundries in the central Bakony Mountains. In the Mecsek Mountains in the south and in the Transdanubian Mountains of the northeast are coal and lignite mines. On the Danube, 43 miles south of Budapest, stands Dunaújváros, Hungary's largest iron and steel center.

Hungary should be rich in antiquities, but the truth is that war has grossly damaged, if not completely destroyed, almost everything of interest that might recall medieval times. One survivor of that period, however, is Székesfehérvár, which in the Middle Ages served several times as the capital of Hungary. Its cathedral, where 36 Hungarian kings were crowned and 15 lie buried, was blown up by the Turks in 1601; the town was rebuilt in the 18th Century and was again demolished during World War II; it has been only partially restored since. Less pretentious monuments have a better chance of survival: not far distant from Székesfehérvár is the town of Várpalota, where close to the towers of the Inota power station may still be found an almost 2,000-year-old marker erected by the engineers of the Roman road that ran from Aquincum, the ancient Roman settlement near Budapest.

Pécs, the old university town in southern Transdanubia, still possesses a four-towered Romanesque cathedral. The Turks, who occupied much of Hungary from 1526 to 1699, converted the structure into a mosque. The Turks also built 12 other mosques in Pécs, surrounded the town with entrenchments and made it one of the most important fortresses of the Ottoman Empire. The jewel of Transdanubia, however, is Lake Balaton, an 8-by-46-mile expanse of clear, tepid water. In the summer its surface is a flutter of white sails, and its beaches are crowded with bathers in bright swimsuits. Around its poplar-lined perimeter, there are charming old churches, abbeys, villas, hotels and taverns.

East of the Danube lies the great Alföld, or plain. This is a vast extense of prairie-flat steppeland broken only by the Tisza River, a slow-moving tributary of the Danube. In the harshness of winter Hungary's rivers can freeze solid, but in the summer heat the *délibab*, a kind of mirage, dances on the distant Alföld horizon. The abundance of sunshine, however, makes possible the cultivation of the Kecskemét apricot, one of the most delicious of the fruits grown in Europe, and of paprika. In the southern regions, particularly in the countryside around Szeged, Kalocsa and Baja, one can see countless bunches of the small paprika peppers drying on trellises, the shiny green cones slowly changing to brilliant carmine in the sun's heat, ready for eventual grinding into powder for packeting and export.

Although the official record says that 96 per cent of all arable land in Hungary has been "socialized," that is, collectivized, or turned into state farms, the fact is that privately owned plots account for 40 per cent of the country's total agricultural production. In many areas a good deal of the traditional country life has been preserved. Horses and cattle are still driven out in the morning and grazed communally. Young men used to summon their herds at evening by blowing on long trumpets, and one is told that this is still done in some parts. Communal ponds outside every village are usually crowded with flocks of snowy geese, guarded by a small girl who appears to have some mysterious rapport with her hissing charges.

During the Turkish occupation the destruction of towns and villages was so widespread that the native inhabitants built only makeshift dwellings, and this custom became so much a part of tradition that even today there is hardly a large or pretentious building (except those erected by the present regime) to be found in the whole area. Most of the low, mud-brick cottages are simply whitewashed, but some peasants prefer to decorate them: the people of the Danube valley use a yellow wash, while on the Romanian frontier one may see a gay fresco

---

HUNGARY: SOME BASIC FACTS

AREA: 35,912 square miles

POPULATION: 10,100,000

MONETARY UNIT: The forint (valued at $.085 at the official exchange rate, about $.04 at the more realistic tourist rate). This book employs the official rate except when noted.

MAJOR EXPORTS: Machinery, consumer goods, food, fuels

RELIGIONS: Roman Catholic, Protestant, Orthodox

here and there. It is still possible to find in the villages one house more imposing than the rest, with a coat of arms carved above the door—the home of the local magnate, who, of course, is no more.

In the Hortobágy steppe area east of the river Tisza, there are large cattle and horse ranches, now state-owned, where Hungarian cowboys called *csikósok* ride the range. They are no longer put on exhibit in rodeos, wearing shovel hats and wide-sleeved blouses, for the entertainment of Western visitors; but when Nikita Khrushchev visited the country in 1964 the *csikósok* kids showed that they could ride as well as Cossacks and presented the Russian Premier with a coach and five white horses.

A CHARACTERISTIC sight on the Alföld is the *gémeskút*, or "crane well," which is distinguished by a tall pole sunk into the ground. On the top of the pole a 12-foot, wedge-shaped beam is balanced. Seen from a distance such a well resembles nothing so much as a huge bird feeding on the plain. The device is a very ancient one, and many of them have gone out of use; nowadays artesian wells supply most of the water, and hundreds of miles of new canals have brought some 250,000 acres of land under irrigation in the eastern areas. The river Tisza, which used to flood vast areas every spring and summer, has been brought under control by some 2,500 miles of levees. Along the river's course are silted-up fens thick with water grasses. Here grow the white water lily, the water buttercup, and the white willows which supply the lithe canes for Hungary's basketwork industry. In the migrating seasons the area near Lake Fehér in the south and the western part of Lake Balaton in Transdanubia are alive with marsh snipe, great white herons, cormorants and other species. On the slopes of the mountains north of the Alföld grow the vines that produce the famous Tokay wines, which used to be called "the king of wines and the wine of kings." Although the kings have departed, Tokay remains a truly regal wine, clear in color, heavy-bodied, not too sweet, but very potent.

If much of Hungary retains a predominantly rural look, the ancient capital of Budapest presents a totally different aspect. Today Budapest is a large, industrial city whose busy managers have not yet grappled with the smoke problem. The city gets its name from two localities, Buda on the west bank of the Danube and Pest on the east. From the heights of Buda one may count a score of baroque and Gothic spires, raised during the city's heyday, but beyond them in the hazy suburbs are many loftier smokestacks, each with its brown plume feathering into the soft mist of smog. Almost two million people live in Budapest, and most of them are satisfied with the air as it is. Smoke means production, work and wages.

Budapest developed rapidly during the Industrial Revolution, and today the city employs 47 per cent of Hungary's factory workers. It is, however, more than a strictly industrial city. Budapest has six universities and 11 colleges and specialized schools. Its 22 municipal districts now cover 202 square miles, yet people still flock to the city, aggravating the acute housing shortage. Despite the construction of 50,000 new apartment units every year, there is still an average of 3.2 persons to each apartment, and 60 per cent of the apartments have only one room. A favorite story in Budapest concerns a schoolboy who, in a class memory test, could not name an object hanging from the wall of his family's apartment "because we only have the middle of the room; other families have the walls." The housing shortage is blamed for the low birth rate and for the popularity of abortion, which is legal in Hungary.

IF a city can be said to have a memory, then Budapest's is a troubled one: it was razed by the Mongols in 1241, destroyed during its reconquest from the Turks in 1686, ravaged in turn by fire and flood, scarred by more than one revolution and shelled in many wars. The marks of violence are everywhere. After the withdrawal of the Mongols in 1242, King Béla IV built the Vár, or fortress, on a defensible elevation in Buda, but he has little to be remembered by because the Wehrmacht made a month-long last stand on the hill in 1945. No trace remains of the splendid Renaissance palace built by the great Hungarian King Mátyás in the 15th Century. Even the Turks, who crushed the weak Jagiełłonian regime in the 16th Century and remained for a century and a half, are represented only by a few fortifications, four public baths, and the tomb of the poet Gül Baba, a dervish in the employ of Suleiman II. The Habsburgs, who were Budapest's chief architectural benefactors, built a palace within the walls of the Vár. It was one of the most sumptuous residences in Europe, but Russian artillery, pounding at the Wehrmacht, reduced it to a ruin and the ancient Vár itself to a heap of rubble.

Considerable restoration has been attempted. Fishermen's Bastion, a rampart traditionally defended by the city's fishermen, looks as new as it should; but the Coronation Church, where later kings of Hungary were crowned, is a blistered cavern inside. The adjoining Jesuit monastery is a hollow shell. The statue of St. Stephen is intact but has the bruised look of an object which has been in a whirlwind. The houses of the living quarter of the Vár have been entirely rebuilt, in some cases with the Gothic façades they are believed to have had originally. Like the Old Town in Warsaw it all has the uncomfortable falseness of a movie set.

If the Government has been tardy about restoration, it is because there were more pressing problems: the war left only one quarter of the city's 40,000 buildings intact. Nor should one begrudge Budapest one of its first postwar constructions: the Liberation Memorial. A huge structure, it is composed of massive stone monoliths, a heroic statue of a Soviet soldier and a 110-foot figure of Liberty. It dominates the city from the Gellért Hill, overshadowing a nearby memorial to St. Gellért, one of the early Christian missionaries in Hungary.

THE Danube is laced with islands where it flows through Budapest. The two major ones are Csepel Island to the south, a major industrial center, and Margaret Island, almost at the city's heart. Named for a devout daughter of King Béla IV who founded a nunnery there, Margaret Island was a hayfield for many years until a Habsburg governor built a pleasure palace on it around 1800. Today the island is still devoted to the pursuit of pleasure, but it now has, as the Communists say, a broader base in the masses. With swimming pools, tennis courts, an open-air opera arena, a casino, restaurants and cafés, the island is beloved by Budapestians, who like to saunter arm in arm on graveled walks among its lawns and flower beds, especially on those summer evenings when the temperature rises over 100°. The poet Gyula Krudy has written: "Not all the engagement notices printed in Pest are so many as the vows of love made under these trees."

There is a thermal spring on Margaret Island that is connected to the heating system of the Grand Hotel, which is located on the island. Budapest's 123 thermal springs contain sulphur, carbonic acid, lime, calcium and salt, as well as other substances. Among the possible beneficiaries may have been the hippopotamuses at the city zoo. They wallowed in these mineral waters after their arrival at the zoo a number of years ago and began breeding vigorously, an unprecedented event in zoological history. Hungary has since been blessed with a valuable export: baby hippos. At the Gellért Hotel, there is a large thermal swimming pool with artificial waves calculated to awake nostalgic memories among the landlocked (and sometimes padlocked) Hungarians.

AN athletic people, the Hungarians excel at water polo, swimming, boxing, wrestling and fencing. Their great passion is soccer. The People's Stadium, an arena completed in 1953 to seat 105,000 spectators, is packed for all big games, such as that of Hungary against Austria. In 1963 a game between Hungary and the U.S.S.R. developed into a riot when the Russian comrades were suspected of foul play. Spectators rushed onto the field and attacked both the Russians and the police. The television broadcast was abruptly cut off, and the sports writers made no mention of the clash in their reports.

Games of chance are forbidden in Hungary, but one can lose a lot of money at bridge, rummy or a whistlike game called *ultimó*. For inveterate gamblers, there is the state lottery, which offers prizes that seem prodigious to Budapestians. While the worker's average monthly wage is 1,700 forints ($145 at the official exchange rate), housing takes only 5 per cent of this, so there are pennies to spare.

The 19th Century is writ large across the inner city of Pest. Houses are uniformly six or seven stories high—pre-elevator height—and there is a system of circular boulevards not unlike those found in Paris. Any resemblance to the French capital is, however, ruled out by the breadth of the Danube. It lacks the intimacy of the Seine, although the Danube also has lovers and fishermen idling on its stony quays.

The river is full of vessels: barges four abreast drawn by powerful tugs, fast hydrofoil ferries, tourist launches of high diesel power, ore boats and tankers from the Black Sea. The seven bridges which crossed the river before the war were demolished by the Germans. Now rebuilt, and with an eighth added since the war, they lend spaciousness to a crowded city. Budapestians are very fond of them, especially of the Lánchid (literally, Suspension Bridge), originally completed in 1849 under the direction of the British engineer Adam Clark. At its anchor points there are four openmouthed bronze lions, and a strictly legendary story goes that when it was pointed out to the sculptor that his lions were tongueless he drowned himself in the river.

The principal buildings on the Pest side—St. Stephen's Basilica, completed in 1868, the Opera House (1884), the National Theater (1875), the National Museum (1847) and perhaps a score of others— are in the neoclassic and Renaissance styles popular a century ago. Their façades, alas, are now covered with factory soot and rubble dust and are marked by not a few bullet holes. If the Habsburgs had intended to make Budapest another Vienna they signally failed; the city misses the *Gemütlichkeit* of the Austrian capital, being too muscular, too much of a frontier town. But before dismissing Budapest as unsophisticated, one would be well advised to visit the National Library, built in 1802, whose stacks hold 1.3 million books, and the Academy of Music (1907), whose staff has included the noted composers Zoltán Kodály and Béla Bartók. The academy has trained such distinguished Hungarian-born American musicians as Eugene Ormándy, Joseph Szigeti and Antal Dorati. In the Fine Arts Museum, there are 14 major rooms devoted to European painting between the 13th and 18th Centuries, with almost every master splendidly represented: Rembrandt, Raphael, Giotto, Titian, Correggio and Dürer, among others.

H OWEVER, the Neo-Gothic Parliament House of 1904 is one of the more pretentious of the world's national assembly halls, its many-spired aspiration hardly measured by the Communist congresses it houses today. The headquarters of the Communist Party, a few blocks away, although almost as large, makes as little appeal to the eye, or mind. At the top of the tree-lined boulevard which leads to City Park, there is a colonnaded crescent of statues representing the country's heroes through a thousand years of history. From this august assembly the Communists expelled, as being too reactionary, the Habsburg rulers Ferdinand I, Karl III, Maria Theresa, Leopold II and Franz Josef. Not far from the colonnade they erected a larger-than-life-size statue of Stalin. He was not to stand there even as long as those earlier heroes, as we shall see.

O NE can learn something from a city's memorials: in Budapest there are kings on horseback, soldiers, saints, statesmen, poets and, more recently, ideal workers; but nowhere can there be so many memorials to rebellion. The city abounds with sculptures of the heroes of resistance to Ottoman rule. There are even more monuments to the leaders of the 1848-1849 revolution against the Habsburgs.

No one was more conscious of the Hungarian tradition of insurgency than Mátyás Rákosi, the Communist Party leader who, with the Soviet Army behind him, took control of Hungary in 1949. The son of a poultry butcher, Rákosi had risen high enough in the Communist Party hierarchy to style himself "Stalin's greatest Hungarian pupil." Indeed, in the psychopathology of both master and pupil, there was a strong element of sadism. Modeling his secret police, the AVH, on Stalin's notorious MGB, successor to the NKVD, Rákosi held down the Hungarians by terror and torture: when Stalin died in 1953, there were 150,000 political prisoners in Hungarian jails and at least 2,000 others had been executed. But with Stalin gone and collective leadership the new vogue in Moscow, the Russians decided that Rákosi's monopoly of power in Hungary should also be broken. In July 1953 Rákosi was forced to surrender the premiership to Imre Nagy, an oldtime Communist but a rather gentle, philosophical man who enjoyed a measure of popularity with the Hungarian people.

As Premier, Nagy launched a "New Course" in Hungary. He improved living conditions for the workers and the peasants by slowing down the expansion of heavy industry and by putting a halt to the collectivization of agriculture by terrorist methods. His most popular policy, however, was the curb he placed on abuses of power by the secret police, the party and the Government. A large number of political prisoners were released, and deportation of prisoners to Russian prison camps was halted.

Rákosi, however, had retained the leadership of the party, and he was by no means pleased by Nagy's growing popularity. Nor was he enamored of Nagy's liberalizing policies. From the start he strove to undermine Nagy and have him deposed. After the ouster of Gyorgy Malenkov as Russia's No. 1 Communist in February 1955, Rákosi succeeded. Nagy was removed from the premiership by Malenkov's successors and was expelled from the Communist Party. Rákosi, with a puppet premier, was again sole ruler of Hungary. But the Hungarian people, having glimpsed a better life under the Nagy premiership, grew more discontented as Rákosi again tried to clamp down tight controls.

IN the ensuing months unrest mounted. At a meeting in June 1956 of the Petöfi Circle, a Communist-sponsored discussion group in Budapest, Mrs. Julia Rajk seized the microphone and demanded that justice be done to her husband, Lászlo Rajk, one of the Communist Party leaders who had been arrested, tried and finally executed after a show trial in 1949. A week later 5,000 to 6,000 people stood all night on the street listening over a loudspeaker to a Petöfi Circle debate in which the Rákosi regime was roundly condemned. When one of the speakers called for the immediate readmission of Imre Nagy to the party, the hall and the crowd outside thundered with applause. The Russians hastily came to the conclusion that Rákosi had to be removed. In his stead, however, they appointed Ernö Gerö, Rákosi's stooge and henchman. A further concession was the "rehabilitation" and proper reburial of Rajk. It was not enough. Some 300 young men marched to the statue of Count Lajos Batthyány, a leading figure in the 1848-1849 revolution, bearing banners calling for "Independence, Liberty."

In October, shortly after the Russians had accepted Władysław Gomułka's solution to the Polish crisis (see Chapter 6), the Hungarian Writers' Association and student groups were refused permission to hold a demonstration in sympathy with the triumphant Poles; a huge crowd gathered near the Duna Hotel at the statue of Sándor Petöfi, the poet of the 1848 revolution. They sang patriotic songs, and an actor recited Petöfi's poem "Magyars Arise!"

A huge concourse of people, including university students and about 800 cadets and officers of the Petöfi Military Academy, gathered in Buda at the statue of General Josef Bem, the Polish commander of one of the 1849 revolutionary armies. There, Péter Veres, president of the Writers' Association, read a seven-point program calling for "an independent national policy" and the return of Nagy to power. The national anthem was sung. Many of the demonstrators carried the red-white-and-green national flag of Hungary, from which the symbol of Communist rule —a hammer and an ear of wheat—had been torn out.

The crowd then drifted across the bridges to Parliament House. Nagy appeared and asked the people to disperse. But when they heard reports of Ernö Gerö's broadcast accusing them of "heaping slanders on the Soviet Union," some of the demonstrators went up to City Park, where they toppled the huge statue of Stalin and dragged it through the streets to the National Theater. There, with much laughter, they hammered it to fragments. Other demonstrators went to the Radio Building in Sándor Street, where they found the AVH in command. They demanded that a list of grievances against the Gerö regime be broadcast. The doors of the Radio Building were slammed, and suddenly the AVH began firing into the mass of people. Some 100 persons were killed. The date was October 23, 1956.

THE news that the AVH had opened fire on the crowd spread rapidly. Workers in the armament plants broke open stores of arms and ammunition and brought truckloads of pistols, rifles and submachine guns to the center of the city. Newly armed citizens began occupying the main squares and halting cars they suspected of carrying AVH personnel. As crowds again gathered in Parliament Square, a cry went up, "We want Nagy," and presently Nagy again appeared on a balcony and received an ovation. That evening Ernö Gerö, acting in concert with the Soviet chief of intelligence in Budapest, declared martial law and asked Russian forces stationed in

Hungary to help put down the revolt. As a concession to the demands, Gerö asked Imre Nagy to take over the premiership. He himself planned to keep actual control by retaining the party leadership.

The next morning Radio Budapest was speaking of "Premier" Nagy and announcing that "Soviet formations stationed in Hungary . . . are taking part in the restoration of order." At pistol point Nagy was forced to tape placatory radio broadcasts. Anastas Mikoyan and Mikhail Suslov, two members of the Soviet Presidium, arrived from Moscow, fired Gerö and installed János Kádár as Party Secretary. It was evidently the Russians' intention to apply to the Hungarian situation the same conciliatory tactics that had been successful in Poland a few days earlier, meanwhile relying on the presence of Soviet tanks to maintain order. But events rapidly got out of hand.

In Parliament Square on October 25 more than 20,000 people were gathered around Soviet tank crews who were being heckled in a friendly way for taking part in an action against their "working-class brothers." From neighboring rooftops AVH guards suddenly opened fire on the crowd, killing between 300 and 800 persons. Enraged citizens stormed the AVH headquarters, and as AVH men came running out with hands raised they were shot. The panicked AVH retaliated by throwing hand grenades into cellars sheltering women and children and, at Magyaróvár, Győr and other provincial centers, massacring hundreds of unarmed civilians. In Budapest, Soviet tanks, moving in to take control of the situation, were shot at and some were destroyed.

At Széna Square, Molotov cocktails found easy targets in tanks unable to maneuver because of barricades placed in the square by the insurgents. On October 27 the Vác prison was broken open, and nearly 1,000 political prisoners were freed. In the village of Felsöpetény, near Budapest, Jozsef Cardinal Mindszenty, Primate of Hungary, who had been imprisoned for seven years, was released by the insurgents. "It is an admirable heroism that is at present

LION AND GRIFFIN, guardians against harm, flank the shield of Budapest. The upper castle represents Pest, the lower Buda. On top rests the traditional symbol of Hungary—the crown of St. Stephen, the first monarch of the Hungarian state.

liberating the fatherland," Mindszenty told foreign news correspondents who had arrived in Budapest.

More political prisoners were freed in an attack on Communist Party headquarters in Republic Square, where there was a sharp battle with AVH officers. Sixty of the police were captured, hanged head downward from trees and beaten to death. Passersby spat on the bodies. There was no looting, nor was there any manifestation of anti-Semitism, despite the fact that Rákosi and others in the terrorist hierarchy were of Jewish origin; mass hatred was directed against the Russians and the AVH. The statue of the Soviet soldier at the foot of the Liberation Memorial on Gellért Hill was heaved from its base by many hands.

By October 30 more than 30 Soviet tanks had been destroyed, and the AVH had been quelled and ordered by Nagy to disband. On that date the Russians started withdrawal of their troops from Budapest, after having informed Nagy's Government of their willingness to negotiate the removal of Soviet forces from all of Hungary. Nagy, no longer under duress, invited those old democratic party leaders who had survived the years of Communist control to join him in forming a new government. The prospect of a democratic Hungary, in which the Communists would inevitably have been routed at the polls, was clearly too much for the Russians to accept. And fortunately for the Russians, the world's attention had already been torn from the Hungarian struggle by the Anglo-French invasion of the Suez Canal.

On November 1 Soviet troops started moving into Hungary—in violation of the Warsaw Pact, the mutual-defense agreement which the Russians had established after the onset of the Cold War as a counter to NATO. When Nagy protested, the Soviet Ambassador claimed that the new troops were intended only to relieve those who had been in the fighting and maintained that Russia was still willing to negotiate the removal of all troops from Hungary. But Soviet forces continued their advance. Late that afternoon Nagy announced that his country was withdrawing from the Warsaw Pact to seek neutral international status. He appealed—in vain—to the United Nations to protect Hungarian neutrality.

On November 4 the Russian forces seized control of strategic airfields, highways and railroads throughout the country. Pál Maléter, Nagy's Minister of Defense, who had as a Hungarian Army colonel stood off Russian attacks on the Kilián Barracks in Budapest only days earlier, was arrested while negotiating with Russian officers. Budapest was attacked.

T HE Hungarian Army and civilian volunteers fought back, but shortages of ammunition halted all organized resistance in the city by the following day. Nagy took refuge in the Yugoslav embassy, but later fell into the hands of the Russians. Cardinal Mindszenty was given asylum in the U.S. Legation. Fighting went on for 10 days in the factory districts of Csepel Island and longer in some provincial areas, but in Budapest the Red Army opened fire even on bread lines. Thousands of young "Freedom Fighters" were deported to the Soviet Union; almost 200,000 Hungarians fled across the Austrian and Yugoslav borders. In the ruins of Budapest Soviet soldiers looted and raped.

A year of virtually direct Soviet rule of Hungary followed. The statue of the Soviet soldier was restored to its place, but not the statue of Stalin. The Government was ostensibly headed by Party Secretary János Kádár, who, shortly before the Soviet suppression of the revolution, had broken with Nagy and formed a Soviet-backed government of his own. Kádár had no power; the population hated him, and the Russians did not fully trust him. Nevertheless, a start was made on reconstruction and housing. Loans and raw materials poured in from the U.S.S.R., and the factories came alive. Soviet occupation troops were gradually withdrawn to barracks outside the cities. In the following years thousands of political prisoners were granted amnesty by the Kádár Government, which gradually gained prestige. Exiles began to drift back, and by June 1958 the revolutionary mood had abated sufficiently for the regime to announce, without fear of disturbance, that Imre Nagy and Pál Maléter had been executed.

Within a decade the revolution had become only a memory. Today the BKH, which has replaced the

AVH as the national security organization, sends a polite note or makes a date in an espresso bar when it has to warn someone against nonsocialist behavior. Political arrests are mostly made for writing slogans on walls. The satirical weekly *Ludas Matyi* carries rasping comments on contemporary life, but refrains from criticism of the leadership—from choice, not by order. Private enterprise has grown to be an important, although limited, sector of the economy. Workers from the collectivized farms are encouraged to cultivate small, private plots, and the produce is sold on free markets. There are more than 50,000 private automobiles; Elizabeth Arden cosmetics, Rhine wines and Scotch whiskies are sold in Váci Street.

Yet it is a strange country, where expelled party members almost outnumber dues-paying party members; where Ernö Gerö is among the unemployed; where the graves of victims of the Stalinist era, like Lászlo Rajk, are virtual shrines. In the U.S. Legation in Budapest Cardinal Mindszenty, alone most nights save for the porter, has learned to speak heavily accented English and occasionally sermonizes visitors.

T HE yellow streetcars, jointed like caterpillars, go rattling by; women conductors, cabdrivers and street sweepers wear baggy, Russian-style trousers. In the arcades aged peasant women bend over lacemaking frames; former aristocrats earn their livings by making deliveries; a onetime baron who used to be a big-game hunter has a job at the zoo. In a little uptown jazz joint teenagers twist madly until, at a signal from the Youth Comrade with the red arm band, the band switches to a fox trot. The Hungarian *csárdás* is danced at dressy balls in the big hotels, but the Gypsy orchestras are sparing with their romance.

In a paneled espresso bar young Hungarian men with strong features and hair growing like manes into their collars sit together, occasionally sipping coffee or white wine, listening not to Gypsy violins, but to a jukebox rendering German Dixieland. There is something about the calculated immobility of this scene which makes returning exiles weep. At 10 o'clock everybody obediently leaves; no city of two million people anywhere in the world can be so quiet as Budapest at night. And yet, life vibrates. As one American visitor remarked: "What a wonderful country this would be if it were free."

An enormous stone lion marks the entrance to a pedestrian walk on Budapest's oldest bridge, which spanned the Danube in 1849.

Hungary's Resilient and Fiercely Proud People

Budapest, having fallen under Soviet domination in 1945 and refallen after a 13-day effort to win freedom in 1956, is unique among Eastern European cities: it has overcome Communist "grayness." Not so gay as it formerly was, Budapest nevertheless still hears violins at night, still swarms with well-dressed girls, still is warmed by the pride of its Magyar people. In the city, Western styles prevail; but rural Hungary —with 60 per cent of the nation's population of 10 million—preserves many of the old Magyar ways.

MANIFOLD DELIGHTS *of chic shops and vibrant night clubs attract many patrons in Budapest*

FASHION SHOW in Budapest's fine Duna Hotel beguiles buyers with dresses that compare favorably with those designed in Paris or Rome, although the materials are often inferior.

SEDATE COFFEE SHOP, the ever-crowded Vörösmarty in Budapest, is now operated by the state, but remains a favorite gathering spot for surviving members of aristocratic families.

BUSY SHOP OWNER rearranges a display of hats in her millinery store on Váci Street, once the Fifth Avenue of the capital. Privately owned shops are still permitted in Hungary.

ACROBATIC ACT amuses the patrons of a Budapest night club *(below)*. Only well-paid Communist officials, professionals and skilled workers can afford such expensive night life.

TWO LOVES, a noble, near-legendary river and a brave history, constitute the poetry of Budapest

MOUNTED MAGYARS on the Millennium Monument in Budapest loom over an honor guard. The statues recall the arrival in Hungary of the Magyars approximately 1,000 years ago.

SPIKED EDIFICE, Budapest's Neo-Gothic Parliament House is seen *(below)* through the arches of another of the city's buildings. Finished in 1904, it has more than 100 large rooms.

LOFTY OBELISK, surmounted by the archangel Gabriel holding the crown of St. Stephen, rises beyond two Budapest girls. The crown was given to Stephen I by the Pope in 1001 A.D.

STATELY RIVER, the 350-yard-wide Danube winds past the delicately lighted buildings of the capital. The two halves of the city, Buda and Pest, are situated on opposite banks of the river.

GATHERING FIREWOOD, a peasant in northern Hungary prepares to load his cart. Hungary suffers from a marked shortage
of coal, oil and natural gas, especially in the countryside.

LOADING GRAPES into a cart, a peasant works during the
harvest. Hungarian wines, and particularly Tokay, are world
renowned. About 80 million gallons are produced each year.

RURAL VILLAGES, *tied to the soil, have shown few changes and seek none*

ENTERING TOWN, a farmer halts his rickety wooden cart on an unpaved road. In their dress, folklore, poetry, music and marriage customs, Hungarian peasants are quite different from their Slav neighbors. Many habits—even their way of cooking with an abundance of cream and spice—can be traced to the Asian steppes, where the Magyars lived for many centuries.

147

9

Economies in Difficulties

IT is one of the ironies of history that Communism came not to the heavily industrialized areas of Europe, where Karl Marx confidently expected his revolution to take place, but to an essentially rural section of the Continent. The Communist society was, after all, to be based on the dictatorship of an industrialized, urban proletariat, and if major industries were lacking, how could there be an industrialized proletariat? The anomaly haunted the first builders of Communism in the Soviet Union, and it haunted the Communist planners of Eastern Europe when they acquired control in the postwar years. As was the case in the Soviet Union the primary goal was to attain the economic and ideological benefits of industrialization as swiftly as possible.

It was not, however, possible to undertake industrialization programs immediately. The harnessing of Eastern Europe's economies to the Nazi war machine, Germany's collapse and the Soviet occupation had left the region in chaos; the new postwar regimes were at first preoccupied with the immediate problems of rehabilitation and survival, but they did rapidly turn their attention to agrarian reform. The Communists, who held varying degrees of power in Poland, Czechoslovakia and Hungary, were enthusiastic proponents of these reforms, although the agrarian programs contradicted Marxist doctrine, which preaches the abolition of private landholding rather than—as was the goal of the land reforms—an expansion in the number of private landholders. In this retreat from Marxist dogma the Communists saw the means of bribing the peasants into neutrality during the crucial stages of the consolidation of Communist power.

AS early as July 1944 the Communist-dominated Polish Government which had arrived in the baggage train of the Red Army decreed the confiscation of all estates larger than 250 acres and of all lands owned by persons claiming German nationality. According to the official figures published by the Communists some 24 million acres of arable land were affected by the decree, and 15 million of these were distributed to individual peasants. Approximately 788,000 new farms were created. The remaining nine million acres were retained by the Government and transformed into state farms which were later to form the base for the socialization of agriculture. It was not until 1949 that the Communists, by then firmly consolidated in power, began to put pressure on the peasants to join the collective farms. The pace of collectivization was slow, however. In spite of economic inducements to merge their farms into collectives, the peasants clung to their own holdings, unwilling to participate in radical experiments which would transform them into regimented agricultural laborers.

Land redistribution was also undertaken in Czechoslovakia—at the expense, in the beginning, of collaborationists and of Czech citizens of German or Hungarian origin. About 7.5 million acres were seized from such people and were distributed among some 122,000 families of Slav origin. The problem of large estates was put aside until 1947, when the Communists, seeking to break the power of the politically influential landowners, forced through parliament a land-reform law which limited individual holdings to 250 acres. After the Communist takeover of the country in 1948 even more land was confiscated. Eventually some 10 million acres, roughly 35 per cent of the total agricultural and forest area of the country, were seized. Only four million acres, however, were redistributed to farmers and landless peasants. With collectivization in mind the state retained the larger share.

A similar course was followed in Hungary. As far as land ownership was concerned Hungary had been virtually a feudal country before World War II; some 40 per cent of the arable land had consisted of private holdings of more than 250 acres. One of the first acts of the Government was to confiscate, without compensation, all estates of more than 1,400 acres. Other large holdings were reduced to a maximum size of 140 acres, and all land owned by persons who had collaborated with the Nazis was seized. A total of eight million acres of agricultural and forest lands was confiscated under the land-reform decree of 1945; more than half of it was distributed to some 640,000 claimants. The state, of course, retained the remainder.

Thus by 1949 the agricultural structures of Poland, Czechoslovakia and Hungary had been radically altered. In each country much of the available land had been redistributed in small parcels while the state retained the rest. With that stage completed the Communist regimes began to press toward collectivization of agriculture. Private farmers were required to sell large amounts of their produce to the state at prices set by the Government. Harassed, in addition, by discriminatory taxes and charged exorbitant rates by the Governments for seed, fertilizer and the use of farm machinery, the peasants of Hungary and Czechoslovakia and, to a lesser degree, those of Poland began to give in. By 1953, 43 per cent of the arable land in Czechoslovakia had been collectivized or turned over to vast, state-owned farms, as had 40 per cent of Hungary's land and some 19 per cent of Poland's.

IN the interim the Communist planners had not forgotten their industrialization goals. As early as 1945 the coalition Governments had begun nationalization of banks, large industrial establishments and foreign trade; by 1949 almost 90 per cent of the industrial labor force in Eastern Europe was employed in industries owned by the state. Now all three countries embarked upon long-range industrialization programs. All their plans aimed at the rapid development of heavy industry; the ultimate aim was to produce in each country a highly industrialized, urbanized and mechanized society possessing a large proletarian majority. The policies all bore resemblances to the line which the Soviet Union had followed since the late 1920s; all were justified by the same theoretical arguments and enforced by the same police-state methods; all served the same objectives. In essence Poland, Czechoslovakia and Hungary —and the other members of the Soviet bloc—were to make themselves over into individual, miniature replicas of the Soviet Union.

During the first few years, progress toward industrialization was quite rapid, according to the official production statistics. The five year development programs launched in 1949-1950 by Poland, Hungary and Czechoslovakia envisaged a quadrupling of industrial output in Hungary and Poland and a doubling in Czechoslovakia's production. To meet the targets, between 40 and 50 per cent of total economic investments was channeled into heavy industry in each country. Steel output, a basic index of industrial activity, grew from 2.6 million metric tons to 4.3 million in Czechoslovakia between 1948 and 1953, from 1.9 million to 3.6 million in Poland and from 770,000 to 1.5 million in Hungary. But as new industrial plants continued to rise throughout the area serious flaws in the economic plans soon came to light.

Insufficient attention had been given to supplying the factories with raw materials, fuel and power. Soviet raw materials at first kept the new industries busy, but as the Soviet's own industrial plant expanded, the demands of its satellites could not be met. Some of the new plants in Poland, Hungary and Czechoslovakia were forced to operate below capacity and even to close down for brief periods.

Absenteeism and high turnover, moreover, caused a drop in labor productivity as the new members of the proletariat grew increasingly discontented with low wages, high production norms and a precipitous

COMMUNIST FARMS: BASIC TYPES

In Eastern Europe, there are three kinds of farms: state, collective and private. On a state farm, which is the preferred type according to Marxist doctrine, the land belongs to the state, and the workers are paid fixed salaries. On a collective farm, members retain ownership of land they contributed when they joined. On some collectives, farmers are remunerated solely on the basis of the amount of land, livestock and farm implements they originally contributed; on others they are paid according to the work performed. On still others a combination of the two payments systems is used. State farms are intended to serve as examples to the peasantry of the advantages of state ownership of the land; in fact, however, state farms in Eastern Europe, as elsewhere in the Communist bloc, operate at heavy losses. Although private farms are usually discriminated against, private holdings—and the small private plots that are allotted to workers on collectives—have been far more productive than state or collective farms in all three Eastern European countries.

decline in the standard of living. By 1952 many of the new industrial plants were failing to meet their production quotas.

Agriculture was in even worse shape. Development plans launched in the late 1940s had looked toward a doubling of agricultural output within five years. The agricultural sector was, however, denied the means to achieve this goal, being allotted only 8 to 12 per cent of total development funds during the period. The drive for collectivization reduced incentives for private farmers, the weather was poor in 1950 and again in 1952, and by 1953 agricultural output in all three countries had not even achieved prewar levels. There were food shortages in the cities. Popular discontent mounted.

After the death of Stalin in 1953, Russia's rulers decided on a "New Course." The drive to collectivize agriculture was temporarily abandoned, and in Hungary and Czechoslovakia some of the collective farms were even disbanded. Some efforts were made to ameliorate living standards. In an attempt to achieve a better balance in the development of the economies, investment in industrial expansion was cut back by more than 50 per cent, and manufacturing targets were scaled down to correspond more realistically with the availability of raw materials. But these measures were undertaken halfheartedly in all three countries, and by 1955 they had been abandoned in favor of a virtual return to the policies of the Stalin era.

Political unrest, combined with exasperation over the long years of economic privation under Communist rule, brought revolt. In June 1956 the workers of Poznań, Poland, rioted in protest against miserable working and living conditions (see Chapter 6). The Hungarian revolution, also in large part economically motivated, took place later that same year. The Russians brutally suppressed the Hungarians and eased the tension in Poland by permitting the installation of a more liberal Communist regime.

The basic economic problem, however, remained. None of the Eastern European countries possessed sufficient raw materials to support an independent national economy. In 1958 Moscow began a new approach by revitalizing the moribund Council for Mutual Economic Assistance, or Comecon, an organization originally conceived as an antidote to the U.S. Marshall Plan. Comecon's new role was to promote a "socialist division of labor" among the Communist-bloc countries, a system under which each of the countries would produce only certain kinds of goods rather than attempt to build a relatively broad-scale economy modeled upon that of the Soviet Union. The plan was to eliminate the duplication of effort and investment which had characterized Eastern Europe's economy as a whole in the postwar years. This scheme, if carried to its logical conclusion, would eventually lead to the establishment of a single, completely integrated, bloc-wide economy directed, planned and managed by some supranational body.

COMECON'S member nations include East Germany, Romania, Bulgaria and Mongolia, as well as the Soviet Union and Poland, Czechoslovakia and Hungary. Comecon plans to allot functions to its members on the basis of natural resources and individual economic traditions. Thus Czechoslovakia is supposed to push forward with its machine-tool industry and the manufacture of electronic equipment and consumer goods. Poland, with its large coal deposits, is to stress mining and the production of chemicals and continue as a meat producer and shipbuilder. Hungary, with bauxite but few other industrial raw materials, is to specialize in consumer goods, precision tools, communications equipment and in other products which require little metal. East Germany is to emphasize power machinery, chemicals and machine tools. Bulgaria is to supply raw materials, chemical products and equipment for light industry. Romania is to be assigned the production of raw materials, particularly petroleum, and the manufacture of equipment for the oil industry.

Only the Soviet Union, with its vast resources, would be permitted to expand its output of all types of products.

The plans are grandiose. But as early as 1962 the Romanians began protesting them; others followed suit. In fact the Comecon integration scheme is still bogged down in declarations of intent; hundreds of experts from the member countries of Comecon are still discussing means of implementing the principle of socialist division of labor.

AN indication of the progress of Comecon's regional-specialization plan can be discovered in the slow growth rate of trade exchanges among the Soviet-bloc partners. The essence of the Comecon program is that each country should concentrate on certain commodities and make its own surpluses available to other nations within the group. If the scheme were working well trade among member countries should be growing at a dynamic rate.

The fact is, however, that trade among the Comecon partners has been increasing at a rate considerably below the mutual trade rate among their most obvious competitors, the Common Market countries of Western Europe. In 1961, for example, the volume of trade among Common Market countries increased by 16 per cent, while trade among the Comecon partners grew by only 10 per cent. In more recent years Comecon's lag behind the Common Market has continued.

Clearly, Comecon's regional-specialization plan is failing, and the reasons for the failure are not difficult to discern. First among them is the similar economic structure of the member countries, a direct result of the policies pursued during the Stalin era. In the main the three nations all require similar raw materials; they have similar goods to sell. A changeover from their autarchic, relatively independent economies would involve enormous sacrifices. Tremendous amounts of work and capital were expended in building the industries and plants of Eastern Europe; the suggestion that his "own" steel mill, however uneconomic, should be dismantled dismays even the most Soviet-oriented Eastern European leader. Moreover, there is a political problem. Heavy-industry plants were touted for a number of years as national status symbols; how does the leader justify to his country the destruction of a symbol of national progress?

Another major reason for Comecon's failure to make significant progress has been the lack of an objective method of determining which country can most efficiently perform a specific production task. The specialization which has developed in the Common Market area has taken place because more efficient producers have been able to undersell their competitors in the market. But within the Soviet bloc it has been impossible to determine comparative costs of production—and thus who is the more efficient producer—because each Communist economy is based on an artificial system of wages and prices established by the arbitrary decisions of the national planning authority. Consequently neither the figures given out as production costs nor the prices of raw materials bear any relation to actual costs. "We not only cannot check the calculations of our partner, or translate our calculations into language which is comprehensible to him, but we have no idea ourselves of the comparable effectiveness of our own production," a Polish economist complained not long ago.

IN recent years the Comecon planners have attempted to deal with this problem by accepting the prices current on the world market—the international "capitalist market" which basically adjudges its dealings in currencies like the U.S. dollar and the British pound—for their own trade exchanges. The adoption of world prices, however, has tended to increase resistance to economic integration within the Communist bloc. Once required to pay world prices for their imports, the countries of Comecon found it more advantageous to buy certain goods from Western sources rather than to accept the generally inferior products manufactured by their Soviet-bloc partners. This tendency, limited only by shortages of hard currency due to inadequate export earnings, has been visible in the Soviet-bloc statistics of recent years. The statistics reveal that the trade of Comecon countries with the West has been growing more rapidly than has trade among the Comecon partners.

It was, however, the attempt to allocate specialized economic tasks to each country which created the greatest conflict among the Comecon countries. The more industrialized countries tried at first to secure more complex and therefore more profitable production assignments, leaving less-developed countries to develop raw-materials production—a long-range program which retards industrialization, requires large expenditures of capital and results in very little initial profit.

IN short, the entire Comecon scheme is riddled with difficulties and conflicts. The basic problem for the Eastern European leaders lies in the contradiction between the obvious economic benefits of specialization and the grave political dangers of too great a dependence on the dominating partner—the Soviet Union. The smaller Comecon countries are acutely aware that each consecutive step toward economic integration not only erodes their economic independence but exposes them more and more to the danger of increased political domination by the Soviet Union.

How much pressure can the Russians exert? The vulnerability of the bloc countries is obvious. Almost all of Hungary's raw materials come from other Comecon countries, and chiefly from the Soviet Union, which supplies three quarters of Hungary's iron ore and more than half of its lumber, coal and oil. Both Poland and Czechoslovakia are heavily dependent on Soviet iron ore and oil.

Only time can tell whether compromises can be effected among the member nations of Comecon, whether they will be able to turn even more to trade with the West, or whether the Soviet Union will attempt to impose its will on its increasingly independent allies.

What is indisputable is that despite shortcomings and gross errors an industrial revolution has taken place in Eastern Europe. The boundary of rural Europe has retreated eastward. Less than two decades after World War II Poland, Czechoslovakia and Hungary were together producing some 20 million tons of steel, more than the output of France, and more than 230 million tons of coal, almost as much as West Germany. Half-enforced, half-spontaneous, the industrialization of Eastern Europe is a new and permanent factor in history, one with vast but as yet unascertainable political implications.

COMPLEX PRODUCTION LINE stretches the length of a room in the Bata Shoe factory in Gottwaldov, Czechoslovakia. Bata is one of the largest makers of shoes in Eastern Europe.

New Efforts to Stimulate Industry

At the end of World War II the Soviet Union found a rich prize in Eastern Europe. Czechoslovakia was one of the most advanced industrial nations in the world. Hungary had a strong agricultural base, and Soviet planners expected to industrialize the country swiftly. German areas acquired by Poland were already industrialized. But planners imposed onerous taxes and de-emphasized consumer-goods production in order to expand heavy industry quickly. Trained managers were replaced by men whose main qualification was loyalty to the Communist regime, and as a result production quotas were often not met. The standard of living plummeted. In an effort to develop agriculture and the production of consumer goods as well as heavy industry, planners have recently launched a drive for total economic integration of the area under an organization known as Comecon. Eastern European nations have resisted Comecon's policies. Now they are looking to the West for new technology and trading opportunities.

WOMEN TECHNICIANS discuss a production problem *(right)* at the Skoda Works in Pilsen, Czechoslovakia. Skoda is a major manufacturer of cars, heavy machinery and munitions.

154

SKILLED WORKERS solder small parts for locomotives at the Skoda Works. Once the industrial leader of Eastern Europe, Czechoslovakia is now only a step ahead of its neighbors.

ELECTRIC LOCOMOTIVE nears completion at the Skoda Works *(below)*. To obtain foreign currency Skoda is currently selling cars cheaply abroad, and charging high prices at home.

TANGIBLE INCENTIVES are taking the place of ideological slogans to encourage production

COMFORTABLE RESIDENCE houses unmarried coal miners in Komló, Hungary. Under new economic policies a growing number of such amenities are being made available to laborers.

SKODA SEDAN is examined by visitors *(below)* to the annual Trade Fair in Brno, Czechoslovakia. This car costs $6,200 in Czechoslovakia, equivalent to two years' wages for a worker.

OFF-DUTY LABORER reads beneath statues honoring Komló miners. While pressing for industrialization, Hungary has increased the production of consumer goods in recent years.

LUXURY HOTEL on the shore of Lake Balaton *(opposite)*, a popular resort area, attracts tourists and wealthier Hungarians: engineers, lawyers, scientists and the managers of industries.

OBSOLESCENT LOCOMOTIVE pulls freight across the Hungarian countryside. Planners, having failed to forge a modern railway system, have begun to import Western equipment.

MASSIVE STEELWORKS at Nowa Huta, Poland, runs at capacity. Output at Nowa Huta, low a few years ago, has been increased by the adoption of Western production techniques.

SMOKING FACTORIES of the Bata Shoe complex *(right)* extend through Gottwaldov, Czechoslovakia. Such large enterprises are now emphasizing research and development programs.

PILLARS OF THE ECONOMY *are being nursed to health by major changes*

VARICOLORED FACADES of the Old Town of Warsaw shine in the afternoon sun as a cruise boat passes down the Vistula. Reduced to rubble during World War II, Warsaw has been largely rebuilt and now has a population of one million.

10

Unsolved Problems

LONG before the abrupt overthrow of Nikita Khrushchev late in 1964 it was apparent that change was again coming to Eastern Europe, as change had so often come before. The house that Josef Stalin built and Khrushchev reconstructed was in considerable disarray. Stalin's attempt to impose an alien Soviet system upon countries with different social and economic bases had ended in failure; Khrushchev, the great revisionist, had not succeeded in making the Communist system work either. Stalin had brutally imposed his will upon his puppets; Khrushchev took power away from the secret police and granted a measure of independence to the once-servile satellites. In so doing he opened the door to a search for "national solutions" to national problems.

In foreign affairs Poland, Czechoslovakia and Hungary have remained reliable allies of the Soviet Union. Each country, in addition, remains a Communist state, utilizing classic Communist methods. Although police terror has been greatly diminished, police control is still the accepted method of enforcing conformity to state policies. Each nation is committed to Marxist goals. Each is still a one-party state, and in each it is the Communist Party that determines the policies of government. But in each, as well, there is far less faith in the infallibility of the leadership of the Soviet Union. In internal and economic matters Eastern Europe has begun to doubt that the Soviet way is the best way, and short of military intervention or the imposition of major economic sanctions, there is no longer any way for the Soviet Union to force Poland, Czechoslovakia and Hungary to accept its dictates.

To say the above is not to declare that life has become easy in Eastern Europe, nor simple for its planners. Major economic problems, like the decline in agricultural production, remain unsolved. Poland's planners would like to increase wheat production by converting the country's numerous small peasant holdings into large state farms or collectives using modern farming methods. But Polish peasants continue to reject socialization and the tractors offered by the producers' cooperatives; they prefer to retain their horses, their land and their independence. It seems unlikely that the Polish Government will attempt to enforce collectivization.

THE Poles face difficulties on other fronts as well. In commerce and industry, there has been widespread unemployment. The Poles have failed to build an efficient, modern industrial system capable of producing high-quality products at competitive prices and of absorbing the surplus labor in the country's agricultural sector. They have announced plans to decentralize economic planning, to give more authority to managers of individual enterprises and to gear production more closely to market demands. But the economy remains stagnant, and the discontent that has arisen from unemployment and the shortage of housing and consumer goods is a continuing problem for the regime. In recent years the Roman Catholic Church, which was briefly freed from Government persecution after Cardinal Wyszyński and his bishops were released in 1956, and which remains the main stumbling block in the Communist path, has again become the object of a campaign of intimidation. Toward the end of 1964 police raided a seminary near Poznań; proceedings were begun to expropriate a seminary near Danzig; and the Wrocław City Council expropriated the residence and offices of the city's archbishop.

The Polish intellectuals, guardians of the Polish culture which constitutes national identity, are being subjected to a series of subtle but effective restrictions. While there is abundant paper on which to print the party literature and even foreign books, a diminishing supply is available for the Polish classics (the works of Adam Mickiewicz, for example, are often out of print) and for the expression, no matter how indirect, of dissatisfaction with contemporary life. A group of writers and artists who in 1964 dared to ask the Government to observe the constitutional guarantees of freedom of expression suffered reprisals to a greater or lesser degree.

THE post-Stalin relaxations initially went very far in Poland—farther than in any other satellite. But in Czechoslovakia, there were no relaxations. There the secret police remained active, and not until a few years ago did their grip begin to loosen. There are still some political prisoners in the jails and Western newspapers are largely unobtainable, but it is now possible to buy once-forbidden novels and to speak relatively freely in public. Most Western radio and television broadcasts are no longer jammed. These steps have not, however, won over Czech youth. They are in a state of rebellion against the regime and openly question past actions, excesses and failures. The regime would like to involve them in political work but admits that it has failed.

But the winds of change are being felt in Czechoslovakia, too. The country is also in economic distress as a result of slavish imitation of the Russian model. The cost of living has soared; industrial output has plummeted. Late in 1964 Czechoslovakia announced that it would drastically overhaul the planning system, encourage competition among plants and make adjustments to the realities of the market. Henceforth the central planners were to confine themselves to establishing over-all guidelines for the development of the economy, instead of drawing up detailed annual plans, and to leave the working decisions to local managers—the most radical departure from the old Soviet system yet to be undertaken in Eastern Europe. An American diplomat stationed in Eastern Europe in 1965 remarked: "The Czechs start everything slower and go much farther than anybody else."

In Hungary no one likes to mention the euphoria of the 1956 revolution and its tragic aftermath. A resigned cynicism and a feeling of noninvolvement with politics are the marks of the country today. The massive aid from the Communist bloc which was pumped into the country after it was brought to heel has stopped, and Hungary's overambitious planning and deficiencies in raw materials made it necessary to cut the goals for industrial growth in half in 1965. But many political prisoners have been released, and more consumer goods are being made available. There is considerable artistic freedom, and life is relatively relaxed. "Why didn't you go to the last meeting of the party?" a Communist asks another in a current joke. "If I'd known it was the last meeting," the friend replies, "I'd certainly have gone."

Even if Hungary is not prosperous, Hungarians are convinced that they know how to live well within limited means; they are proud of the relative liberality of their regime compared with those of other nations within the Communist bloc, and they are convinced that there will be no return to the terrors of the Stalin era—but they are careful when they state such convictions to make certain of their listeners. Hungary, like the rest of Eastern Europe, is well aware that Soviet troops are still stationed within the region.

It is one thing to state that the era of bloody Soviet repression is past; it is quite another to forget the presence of those troops, of the proximity of the Soviet Union, of the continuing importance to Eastern Europe of Soviet oil, raw materials and foodstuffs. The Soviet Union has never been reluctant to use power to advance its ends. After half a century of civil war, invasion, famine, blood purge and world war it has made itself into the world's second-greatest industrial nation. Russian national goals are as important in Russian minds as is Marxist ideology. The Communists of Eastern Europe are unlikely to forget that fact.

THE Communists who have run the affairs of Eastern Europe in recent years are men of a certain toughness of fiber and, one would add, turgidity of mind, for whom power has an unrivaled appeal—and who realized that it was only through an acceptance of Communism and its ostensible goals that a man could attain power. They have long exercised direction, through the party, of every area of national life—finance, foreign affairs, economic planning, defense, public order, law, security, propaganda, education, culture and the arts, labor relations, industry, agriculture. Theirs is not a secure world; in the Communist system failure means anathema and obloquy as well as loss of income and privilege. There are men who thrive in this atmosphere. The rewards for those who do get to the top are great: uncounted privileges, luxurious living and an enjoyment of power unmatched in democratic countries by men of equal capacity.

THEY may be glimpsed, these party bureaucrats, in the private dining rooms of the big Orbis, Cedok and IBUSZ hotels in Warsaw, Prague and Budapest. They are endlessly conferring—regional and district chiefs, directors of industry, commerce, transport. They are men of watchful solemnity, with conference-table voices. Their statements are careful and precise, like those of all-night poker players. Comparisons between them and capitalist businessmen cannot be made: the flush of vodka does not lead to laughter and raillery; Communist managers are not really free men. Many of them are of peasant origin and bring to their present stations something of peasant hardness, durability and suspicion.

Today the old-line Communist bureaucrats are fighting a rear-guard action against a new, younger generation of skilled managers, engineers and economists who are aware of the failures of the Communist system and who want recognition of their own talents and abilities. One of the chief defects of the system is that it has long put conformity above competence; party hacks have been more likely to advance than have rebels from the party line. "The old system of planned management leaves behind it a highly unsatisfactory state of affairs as regards the qualifications of leading executives," wrote the Czech economist Radoslav Selucký in the official organ of the Communist Youth League, *Mladá Fronta*, in 1964. "At the present time only 12.3 per cent of the directors of the Czechoslovak industrial enterprises and plants have a university education, while 31.4 per cent of the directors possess only an elementary education. Although in other leading jobs—those of deputy directors, heads of individual organizations and production units—the situation is slightly better, the number of those without any specialist education in these crucial posts is also disproportionately high."

The old-line Communist bureaucrat, despite an inexhaustible dedication, is neither imaginative nor flexible. It has never occurred to him that socialist slogans do not cure national ills. The announcements of decentralization in economic planning and of the adoption of Western techniques in 1964 and 1965 represented a victory for the new group of managers and technicians. How long the old-line bureaucrats will be able to withstand the pressure from those concerned with getting the job done, rather than advancement on the basis of the latest shift in the party line, is a question yet impossible to answer.

OBSERVERS who are far away say: "Very few of the people are real Communists; in free elections they would be defeated." This is a banality in the ears of Eastern Europe, and for the West one of the most deceptive and dangerous of ideas. For there can be no free elections. Eastern Europe is for the foreseeable future inexorably linked to the Soviet Union. Efforts to increase trade and cultural contacts between the region and the West, however successful, will not break the chain. Eastern Europe is Russia's prey. Clearly Russia regards the region as its reward for its role in the defeat of Germany.

Whenever circumstances bring men close to danger, they tread with care, although distant bellowings may boast the contrary. There was no real way, for example, in which the West could have aided the Hungarians in 1956 without risking holocaust. There is no sign that the Soviet Union is in danger of collapsing from fright; the wit and resource of its fund of leaders seem likely to keep the world bemused for some time to come.

Eastern Europe is resigned to the fact of Soviet power and of Soviet goals. Its peoples are tenacious and enduring. Hardship they have always known, and oppression more often than liberty, which makes liberty the more precious; few peoples understand better the possibilities inherent in changing political situations. They have already moved away from total Soviet direction; they may yet move farther.

In some matters they are likely to remain committed to Soviet policies. At the end of World War II millions of Germans were expelled from Poland and Czechoslovakia. The resulting fears and suspicions were no doubt foreseen by the Soviet leaders—and welcomed by them, since the tension made reconciliation between Germany and its Slav neighbors difficult, if not impossible. Both Poland and Czechoslovakia are now forced to look eastward for their support rather than westward. The Government of Poland, quite apart from Communist loyalties, continues to support the existence of the artificial East Germany because the status quo indirectly guarantees Poland's own borders. The fear that revitalized Germany might someday return to claim the lands ceded to Poland after the war is very real. Such fears help to explain the implacable opposition of Eastern Europeans to the creation of a multinational nuclear force in Western Europe which would include West Germany. The thought of Germans with atomic bombs is a nightmare in the mind of Eastern Europe.

WHATEVER its difficulties, Eastern Europe itself remains both strange and beautiful. Lake and forest, plain and mountain seem older than similar configurations in Western Europe. And yet there is distance and emptiness, space which makes one think of the American Northwest. The region has been long lived in; the impact of an ancient humanity is evident in the planting of villages in windless folds of hill and dale and the stones that show the mark of man on so many craggy summits. The great forests are very still, and the sun's light striking at an oblique angle between the regularly spaced rows of trees gives the impression of a Gothic plan which the cathedral makers may have tried to imitate. Nor have the forest and lakeland animals retreated from man, but seem to have arrived at some kind of balance with him. Man, in return, seems to have struck a balance with nature: the farm with its fleecy and feathered dependents exists; the horse, at least in Poland, is still man's patient friend.

Yet a traveler leaves Eastern Europe with a feeling of sadness. The whole movement of Europe is toward integration and the destruction of barriers between nations; Eastern Europe still lies behind the Iron Curtain. The Curtain, to be sure, is not so rigid as it once was. But it has yet to disappear.

Two soldiers in Warsaw pass an ornate doorway whose heroic statues bear bullet scars from street fighting during World War II.

VIOLENCE AND HARDSHIP have long been the lot of Eastern Europeans . . .

Hungarian girls keep trim with track-and-field sports in Pioneer Stadium on Margaret Island in Budapest.

One of Czechoslovakia's many satirical theater groups gives an uninhibited performance (opposite) in Prague

. . . yet they have been able to minimize misfortune through an appreciation of simple

pleasures and, in their artistic vitality, show an ever-renewing independence of spirit

Appendix

HISTORICAL DATES

A.D. 1st-6th Centuries — Eastern Europe becomes the scene of numerous migratory movements. During the Sixth Century, Slav groups settle in the area of present-day Czechoslovakia

9th Century — The Moravian Empire is formed by the Slav Czechs of Bohemia and Moravia and the Slovaks of Slovakia

896 — A non-Slav people known as the Magyars settle in the middle Danube basin in present-day Hungary. Driving a wedge between the western and eastern Slavs, they soon extend the Hungarian state to frontiers which endure until 1918

10th Century — The Slav tribes of the Vistula and Oder basins are united under the Piasts, founders of the Polish state. The Moravian Empire collapses under German and Magyar attacks. Bohemia and Moravia come under the rule of a native Bohemian dynasty, the Přemyslid

1240-1242 — Mongols raid Poland and Bohemia, devastate Hungary

1253-1278 — Bohemia reaches the height of its power under Přemysl II, extending from the Oder River to the Adriatic. But after his death Bohemia loses much of the realm to the Habsburgs of Austria

1301 — With its native Arpád dynasty extinct, Hungary's crown passes to foreign rulers

1310 — The rule of Bohemia passes to the House of Luxembourg

1333-1370 — Under the rule of Casimir the Great, Poland enjoys a period of prosperity

1386 — As Poland and Lithuania join in a political union, the Jagiełłonian dynasty replaces the Piast on the Polish throne

1400-1415 — John Hus, a Czech Roman Catholic cleric, publicly advocates Church reforms. Delivered to the Church Council at Constance, he is tried and burned as a heretic

1410 — Poles and Lithuanians defeat the Teutonic Knights at the Battle of Grunwald

1415-1434 — The rise of the Hussite religious and nationalistic movement leads to war between Hussites and Roman Catholic Germans

1526 — The crowns of Bohemia and Hungary pass to the Habsburgs

1526-1699 — Turkish invaders defeat the Hungarians. Hungary is divided into three parts: center and south are under direct Turkish rule; Transylvania is semi-autonomous; Royal Hungary is ruled by the Habsburgs

1618 — Czech nobles revolt against the Habsburgs

1620 — The Czech nobles are defeated at the Battle of the White Mountain

1654-1667 — Poland and Lithuania become embroiled in wars with the Cossacks of the Ukraine, Russia and Sweden and lose large amounts of territory

1683 — King Jan Sobieski of Poland and his army save Vienna from invading Turks and help liberate Hungary from the Turks

1699 — Turks withdraw from Hungary, whose territory comes under Habsburg rule

18th Century — Dissension increases between the Magyars and other elements in Hungary. Attempts by the Austrian Crown to improve the condition of the peasantry are blocked by the landowners. In Bohemia the Crown introduces social reforms, but attempts to Germanize the Czechs provoke a revival of nationalism

1772-1795 — Under Poland's last King, Stanislas Augustus Poniatowski, Poland succumbs to three successive partitions by Russia, Prussia and Austria

1807 — As a result of Napoleon's victory over Russia, Prussia and Austria, Poland recovers part of its lost territories

1815 — The Congress of Vienna redefines Polish borders, but the country is in effect ruled by Russia

1830-1831 — The Poles rebel unsuccessfully against foreign rule

1848-1849 — A movement for internal reform and independence from Austria comes to a head in Hungary. Lajos Kossuth proclaims independence, but aid from Russia enables the Habsburgs to reimpose their rule

1863 — Poland again unsuccessfully revolts against foreign rule

1867 — Hungary gains independence from Austria in internal matters. The two countries agree to collaborate in defense and foreign affairs and to share the same monarch

1871-1918 — The Czechs' desire for independence from Austria-Hungary mounts

1918 — With the defeat of Germany and Austria-Hungary in World War I and the collapse and Bolshevization of Russia, Poland regains independence. The new state of Czechoslovakia is formed. Hungary breaks its ties with Austria. The Habsburgs are dethroned

1919 — Admiral Miklós Horthy becomes Regent of Hungary and rules until 1944

1919-1938 — Czechoslovakia flourishes economically and politically but is troubled by dissatisfactions among its many minority groups

1926 — Józef Piłsudski becomes virtual dictator of Poland. After his death in 1935 his military collaborators rule the country

1938 — The Munich Pact forces Czechoslovakia to surrender the Sudetenland to Germany

1939 — World War II begins as Germany invades Poland

1941 — Hungary joins the Axis

1944-1945 — Soviet troops rout Germans in Poland, Hungary and most of Czechoslovakia and occupy all three countries. Poland's area is reduced and its borders are shifted westward

1947-1948 — Russian support enables Communists to seize power in the Eastern European countries

1948-1952 — The defection of Yugoslavia from the Soviet bloc provokes extensive purges in Eastern Europe's Communist Parties

1953-1955 — After the death of Stalin, there is some relaxation of Communist control in Eastern Europe

1956 — Poland's economic and political ills lead to a change of leadership. The country gains a measure of independence from Soviet Russia. The Hungarian revolution is suppressed by Soviet troops

1956-1965 — Within a political framework still dominated by the Soviet Union, Poland, Czechoslovakia and Hungary endeavor to improve shaky economic conditions while attempting to acquire some independence in cultural and economic areas

FOR FURTHER READING

CHAPTER 1: THE TROUBLED LANDS

Busek, Vratislav, and Nicolas Spulber, *Czechoslovakia*. Frederick A. Praeger, New York, 1957.

Cross, Samuel Hazzard, *Slavic Civilization through the Ages*. Russell & Russell, Inc., New York, 1963.

East Europe. A Monthly Review of East European Affairs. Free Europe Committee.

Halecki, Oscar, ed., *Poland*. Frederick A. Praeger, New York, 1957.

Helmreich, Ernst C., ed., *Hungary*. Frederick A. Praeger, New York, 1957.

Motka, Leo, and Authors Collective, *Touring Czechoslovakia*. Sports and Tourism Publishing House, Prague, 1962.

Wanklyn, Harriet, *Czechoslovakia*. Frederick A. Praeger, New York, 1954.

CHAPTERS 2 AND 3: CENTURIES OF GROWTH AND STRUGGLE

Crankshaw, Edward, *The Fall of the House of Habsburg*. The Viking Press, New York, 1963.

Dvornik, Francis, *The Slavs in European History and Civilization*. Rutgers University Press, 1962.

Glaser, Kurt, *Czecho-Slovakia, a Critical History*. The Caxton Printers, Ltd., Caldwell, Idaho, 1961.

Halecki, O., *A History of Poland*. Roy Publishers, New York, 1956.

Krofta, Dr. Kamil, *A Short History of Czechoslovakia*. Robert M. McBride & Company, New York, 1934.

Lengyel, Emil, *1,000 Years of Hungary*. John Day Company, New York, 1958.

Macartney, C. A., *Hungary: A Short History*. Aldine Publishing Company, Chicago, 1962.

Mizwa, Stephen P., ed., *Great Men and Women of Poland*. Macmillan, New York, 1942.

Reddaway, W. F., J. H. Penson, O. Halecki and R. Dyboski, eds., *The Cambridge History of Poland*. (2 vols.) Cambridge University Press, 1950 and 1941.

Seton-Watson, R. W., *A History of the Czechs and Slovaks*. Hutchinson & Co., Ltd., London, 1943.

Strakhovsky, Leonid I., *A Handbook of Slavic Studies*. Harvard University Press, 1949.

Thomson, S. Harrison, *Czechoslovakia in European History*. Princeton University Press, 1953.

CHAPTER 4: WORLD WARS AND COMMUNIST TAKE-OVER

Beneš, Eduard, *Memoirs*. Houghton Mifflin, Boston, 1954.

Borsody, Stephen, *The Triumph of Tyranny*. Macmillan, New York, 1960.

Buell, R. L., *Poland, Key to Europe*. Knopf, New York, 1939.

Fejtö, François, *Behind the Rape of Hungary*. D. McKay, New York, 1957.

Freidin, Seymour, *The Forgotten People*. Charles Scribner's Sons, New York, 1962.

Kertesz, S. D., *The Fate of East Central Europe*. University of Notre Dame Press, 1956.

Komarnicki, Titus, *Rebirth of the Polish Republic*. Heinemann, London, 1957.

Macartney, C. A., *A History of Hungary, 1929-1945*. (2 vols.) Frederick A. Praeger, New York, 1956.

Piłsudski, Józef, *Memoirs of a Polish Revolutionary Soldier*. Faber & Faber, London, 1931.

Ripka, Hubert, *Czechoslovakia Enslaved*. V. Gollancz, London, 1950.

Schmitt, B. E., ed., *Poland*. University of California Press, 1945.

CHAPTER 5: IN COMMUNISM'S GRIP

Dziewanowski, M. K., *The Communist Party of Poland: An Outline of History*. Harvard University Press, 1959.

Hiscocks, Richard, *Poland: Bridge for the Abyss?* Oxford University Press, 1963.

Korbel, Josef, *The Communist Subversion of Czechoslovakia. 1938-1948*. Princeton University Press, 1959.

Seton-Watson, Hugh, *The East European Revolution*. (3rd ed.) Frederick A. Praeger, New York, 1956.

Staar, Richard F., *Poland, 1944-1962: The Sovietization of a Captive People*. Louisiana State University Press, 1962.

Taborsky, Edward, *Communism in Czechoslovakia, 1948-1960*. Princeton University Press, 1961.

Ulam, Adam, *Titoism and the Cominform*. Harvard University Press, 1952.

CHAPTER 6: POLAND

Komorowski, T. (General Bór), *The Secret Army*. Macmillan, New York, 1951.

Lane, Arthur Bliss, *I Saw Poland Betrayed*. Bobbs-Merrill, New York, 1948.

Lewis, Flora, *A Case History of Hope*. Doubleday, New York, 1958.

Małisz, Bolesław, *Poland Builds New Towns*. Polonia, Warsaw, 1962.

Mikołajczyk, Stanisław, *The Rape of Poland*. Whittlesley House, New York, 1948.

Uszyńska, Zofia, ed., *Poland, Travel Guide*. Agpol, Warsaw, 1960.

Zurawski, J. W., *Poland, The Captive Satellite*. Endurance Press, Detroit, 1962.

CHAPTER 7: CZECHOSLOVAKIA

Czechoslovakia. The Nagel Travel Guide Series, Les Editions Nagel, Geneva, 1959.

Kállay, Karol, *Slovakia, Yesterday and Today*. Artia, Prague, 1961.

Plicka, Karel, *Prague in Photographs*. Artia, Prague, 1961.

Praha Guidebook. Sports and Tourism Publishing House, Prague, 1960.

Schmidt, Dana Adams, *Anatomy of a Satellite*. Little, Brown and Company, Boston, 1952.

Tapié, Victor-Lucien, *The Age of Grandeur, Baroque Art and Architecture*. Grove Press, New York, 1960.

CHAPTER 8: HUNGARY

The Editors of *Survey*, *Hungary Today*. Frederick A. Praeger, New York, 1962.

Halász, Zoltán, ed., *Hungary: A Comprehensive Guidebook*. Corvina Press, Budapest, 1956.

Huba, Lászlo, Bela Markos, and others, *Budapest: A Guide Book*. Corvina Press, Budapest, 1959.

Pécsi, Márton, and Béla Sárfalvi, *The Geography of Hungary*. Corvina Press, Budapest, 1964.

Váli, Ferenc A., *Rift and Revolt in Hungary*. Harvard University Press, 1961.

CHAPTER 9: THE ECONOMY

Alton, Thad Paul, *Polish Postwar Economy*. Columbia University Press, 1955.

Balassa, Bela A., *The Hungarian Experience in Economic Planning: A Theoretical and Empirical Study*. Yale University Press, 1959.

Michal, Jan M., *Central Planning in Czechoslovakia*. Stanford University Press, 1960.

Montias, John Michael, *Central Planning in Poland*. Yale University Press, 1962.

Spulber, Nicolas, *The Economics of Communist Eastern Europe*. John Wiley & Sons, Inc., New York, 1957.

Wszelaki, Jan, *Communist Economic Strategy: The Role of East Central Europe*. National Planning Association, Washington, D.C., 1959.

Zauberman, Alfred, *Industrial Progress in Poland, Czechoslovakia, and East Germany, 1937-1962*. Oxford University Press, 1964.

CHAPTER 10: UNSOLVED PROBLEMS

Brzezinski, Zbigniew K., *The Soviet Bloc: Unity and Conflict*. (Rev. ed.) Frederick A. Praeger, New York, 1961.

East Central Europe and the World: Developments in the Post-Stalin Era. University of Notre Dame Press, 1962.

Fischer-Galati, Stephen, *Eastern Europe in the Sixties*. Frederick A. Praeger, New York, 1963.

Wiskemann, Elizabeth, *Germany's Eastern Neighbours. Problems Relating to the Oder-Neisse Line and the Czech Frontier Regions*. Oxford University Press, 1956.

FAMOUS EASTERN EUROPEAN CULTURAL FIGURES AND THEIR PRINCIPAL WORKS

Cosmas	1045-1125	Czech. First chronicler of Czech history and founder of Czech historiography
Stitný, Thomas	1333-1405	Czech. Author of religious treatises; also propagated the use of Czech over Latin
Hus, John	c.1370-1415	Czech. Religious thinker, preacher, writer: *De Ecclesia*. Also reformer of Czech orthography: *De Ortographia Bohemica*
Chelčický, Peter	1390-1460	Czech. Radical social thinker and pacifist; spiritual father of the Bohemian Brethren
Rej, Mikołaj	1505-1569	Polish. Known as the father of Polish literature, he was one of the first Polish writers to turn from Latin to the vernacular: *Life of an Honest Man*
Kochanowski, Jan	1530-1584	Polish. Great poet of the Polish renaissance: *Laments*
Balassa, Bálint	1554-1594	Hungarian. Greatest lyrical poet of his time: *Farewell to My Love*
Komensky, Jan Amos (Comenius)	1592-1670	Czech. Author and educational reformer: *Orbis Sensualium Pictus*
Sarbiewski, Maciej Kazimierz (Sarbievius)	1595-1640	Polish. One of the greatest Latin poets of relatively recent times, he is known as the "Christian Horace": *Odes*
Bessenyei, György	1748-1811	Hungarian. Comedy: *The Philosopher*. Poetry: *King Matthias*
Dobrovský, Josef	1753-1829	Czech. Scholar, writer; codifier of the revived Czech language
Kisfaludy, Sándor	1772-1844	Hungarian. Poetry: *Plaintive Love*
Csokonai, Mihály Vitéz	1773-1805	Hungarian. Lyrical poetry: *Dorothy*
Jungmann, Josef	1773-1847	Czech. Philologist, critic, poet and translator. Creator of modern Czech as a literary language. His greatest achievement was the compilation of a Czech-German dictionary
Kisfaludy, Károly	1788-1830	Hungarian. His tragedies mark the beginning of Hungarian drama: *Irene*
Kölcsey, Ferenc	1790-1838	Hungarian. Poet and critic. Author of the Hungarian national hymn. Poetry: *Vanitatum Vanitas*
Kollár, Jan	1793-1852	Slovak. Poet who wrote mostly in Czech: *The Daughter of Sláva*
Safařík, Pavel Josef	1795-1861	Slovak. Philologist and leading figure in the revival of the Czech and Slovak languages
Mickiewicz, Adam	1798-1855	Polish. Regarded as the country's greatest romantic poet and playwright. His *Pan Tadeusz* and other works exerted an influence upon all future generations
Palacký, František	1798-1876	Czech. Historian who contributed enormously to the revival of Czech national aspirations. Also active as politician: *History of Bohemia*
Vörösmarty, Mihály	1800-1855	Hungarian. Poet known for his historical epics: *Zalán's Defeat*
Słowacki, Juliusz	1809-1849	Polish. Romantic poet and a master of the Polish language: *Balladyna, Pan Beniowski*
Mácha, Karel Hynek	1810-1836	Czech. Romantic poet, undoubtedly greatest in the Czech language: *May*
Kraszewski, Józef	1812-1887	Polish. Prolific novelist with several hundred volumes to his credit. Considered the father of the Polish novel: *Jermola, An Old Tale*
Stúr, Ludevít	1815-1856	Slovak. Poet and author. Founder of the Slovak literary language and modern Slovak literature
Arany, János	1817-1882	Hungarian. Great romantic poet. Many of his poems are based on historical topics: *Toldi*
Němcová, Božena	1820-1862	Czech. Novelist: *The Grandmother*
Petöfi, Sándor	1823-1849	Hungarian. Revered poet and patriot: "Magyars Arise!"
Madách, Imre	1823-1864	Hungarian. Poet and dramatist: *The Tragedy of Man*
Jókai, Mór	1825-1904	Hungarian. Popular novelist, essayist and critic. Major novel: *Other Times, Other People*
Neruda, Jan	1834-1891	Czech. Essayist and poet: *Tales of the Old Quarter, Ballads and Romances*
Sienkiewicz, Henryk	1846-1916	Polish. Historical novelist: *Quo Vadis, With Fire and Sword*. Winner of the Nobel Prize for literature in 1905
Országh-Hviezdoslav, Pavel	1849-1921	Slovak. Often called the greatest Slovak poet: *The Gamekeeper's Wife*
Jirásek, Alois	1851-1930	Czech. Historical novelist: *Temno*
Vrchlický, Jaroslav	1853-1912	Czech. Poet, translator and playwright. Play: *The Night on the Karlštejn*. Poetry: *Gods and the People*
Conrad, Joseph (Korzeniowski, Josef)	1857-1924	Polish. Novelist and patriot. Gained world fame by his seafaring novels and stories written in English: *Lord Jim, The Shadow Line*. Political novel: *Under Western Eyes*
Reymont, Władysław	1867-1925	Polish. Novelist: *The Peasants*. Winner of the 1924 Nobel Prize for literature
Molnár, Ferenc	1878-1952	Hungarian-born playwright: *The Swan*. Also novelist: *The Paul Street Boys*
Hašek, Jaroslav	1883-1923	Czech. Journalist and novelist: *The Good Soldier Schweik*
Kafka, Franz	1883-1924	Czech-born author: *The Trial*
Capek, Karel	1890-1938	Czech. Novel: *War with the Newts*. Drama: *R.U.R., The White Sickness*
Dąbrowska, Marja	1892-	Polish. Novelist: *Nights and Days*
Wankowicz, Melchior	1892-	Polish-born novelist and short-story writer: *The Battle of Monte Cassino*
Wierzyński, Kazimierz	1894-	Polish. Poet: *Olympic Laurel*
Słonimski, Antoni	1895-	Polish. Essayist, literary critic and poet: *The Judgment of Don Quixote*
Németh, Laszlo	1901-	Hungarian. Novelist, playwright and essayist. Drama: *The Two Bolyais*
Seifert, Jaroslav	1901-	Czech. Perhaps the best Czech poet now living: *Mother*
Illyés, Gyula	1902-	Hungarian. Poet and author: *The People of the Puszta*
Novomesky, Laco	1904-	Slovak. Political figure and poet: *Villa Tereza*
Koestler, Arthur	1905-	Hungarian-born novelist and political writer: *Darkness at Noon, Thieves in the Night*
Ważyk, Adam	1905-	Polish. Poet. His "Poem for Adults" helped precipitate the 1956 revolution
Kolakowski, Leszek	1927-	Polish. Communist revisionist, philosopher and playwright: *Entrance and Exit*
Hlasko, Marek	1932-	Polish. Novelist: *The Cemetery, The Eighth Day of the Week*

MUSIC

Mysliveček, Josef	1737-1781	Czech. Composed operas and symphonic, chamber and orchestral works. Opera: *Bellerofonte*
Chopin, Frédéric	1810-1849	Polish. The country's greatest composer. Polonaises, mazurkas, *Concerto in E minor, Op. 11*
Erkel, Ferenc	1810-1893	Hungarian. Composer of the Hungarian national anthem. Operas: *Hunyadi László, Bánk Bán*
Liszt, Franz	1811-1886	Hungarian. The country's greatest composer and pianist. Hungarian rhapsodies, préludes, *Liebesträume*
Moniuszko, Stanisław	1819-1872	Polish. Composer of popular works and founder of the Polish national opera. *Halka*
Smetana, Bedřich	1824-1884	Czech. Composer who raised Czech music to its greatest creative heights. Operas: *The Bartered Bride, Libuše*. Symphonic poems: *My Country*. Chamber music: *From My Life*
Dvořák, Antonín	1841-1904	Czech. Prolific composer: *Stabat Mater, Requiem, From the New World, Humoresque*
Janáček, Leoš	1854-1928	Czech. Composer of operas and other orchestral works. Opera: *Jenufa*
Paderewski, Ignace Jan	1860-1941	Polish. Great pianist and composer: *Minuet in G, Symphony in B minor*. Opera: *Manru*
Landowska, Wanda	1877-1959	Polish harpsichordist
Bartók, Béla	1881-1945	Hungarian. Composer: *Duke Bluebeard's Castle, Cantata Profana, Music for Strings, Percussion Instruments, and Celesta*
Kodály, Zoltán	1882-	Hungarian. Choral compositions: *Psalmus Hungaricus, Te Deum of Budavár*. Opera: *Háry János*
Martinů, Bohuslav	1890-1959	Czech composer. Opera: *The Marriage*
Hába, Alois	1893-	Czech. Composer of wide range and style, expert in quarter-tone and sixth-tone music. Opera: *The Mother*
Farkas, Ferenc	1905-	Hungarian composer. Comic opera: *The Magic Cupboard*
Lutoslawski, Witold	1913-	Polish. Pianist and composer: *Concert for an Orchestra, Little Suite, Polish Dances*

PAINTING AND SCULPTURE

Ferenczy, István	1792-1856	Hungarian. Sculptor whose works are fine examples of classicist style: *The Shepherd Girl*
Michałowski, Piotr	1801-1855	Polish. One of the great painters of horses and of military scenes: *Battle of Somo Sierra*
Grottger, Arthur	1837-1867	Polish. Painter famous for his sketches inspired by the 1863 uprising
Matejko, Jan	1838-1893	Polish. The country's greatest historical painter: *Battle of Grunwald*
Von Munkáscy, Mihály	1844-1900	Hungarian. Painter who was a master of 19th Century European pictorial art
Kupka, František	1871-1957	Czech. Abstract painter, satirist and illustrator
Svabinsky, Max	1873-1962	Czech. Painter and portraitist. His work also included woodcuts, mosaics and stained-glass windows of St. Vitus' Cathedral, Prague
Stursa, Jan	1880-1925	Czech. Leading modern sculptor: *The Wounded Man*
Stróbl, Zsigmond Kisfaludy	1884-	Hungarian. Sculptor whose statues ornament several points in Budapest, the best-known of them being the Liberation Memorial on Gellért Hill
Trnka, Jiří	1912-	Czech. Puppeteer. Film: *The Emperor and the Nightingale*
Brzozowski, Tadeusz	1918-	Polish abstractionist
Kierzkowski, Bronislaw	1924-	Polish. Modern painter
Lebenstein, Jan	1930-	Polish. Modern painter of idol-like, heavily textured figures

SCIENCE

Copernicus, Nicholas	1473-1543	Polish. Astronomer. Major work: *De Revolutionibus Orbium Coelestium*
Purkinje, Johannes Evangelista	1787-1869	Czech. Pioneer in experimental physiology, histology and embryology
Ressel, Josef Ludwig Franz	1793-1857	Czech. Inventor of screw propeller for steamships
Semmelweis, Ignaz	1818-1865	Hungarian. Physician who discovered cause of puerperal fever
Wróblewski, Zygmunt	1845-1888 }	Polish scientists. They were the first to liquefy oxygen and other gases
Olszewski, Karol	1846-1915 }	
Eötvös, Roland	1848-1919	Hungarian. Physicist who invented an instrument called the Eötvös balance, which is used to determine variations of gravity to detect the location of subterranean materials
Curie, Marie Skłodowska	1867-1934	Polish. Co-discoverer of radium and recipient of two Nobel Prizes (in physics, 1903, and chemistry, 1911)
Malinowski, Bronislaw	1884-1942	Polish. One of the world's most distinguished anthropologists. Works: *Argonauts of the Western World, The Sexual Life of Savages in Northwest Melanesia*
Von Hevesy, George	1885-	Hungarian. Nobel laureate in biochemistry (1943), for developing radioactive isotopes as laboratory tracers in research on chemical processes
Heyrovský, Jaroslav	1890-	Czech. Country's first Nobel Prize winner (in physical chemistry, 1959) for developing polarographic methods of chemical analysis
Szent-Györgyi von Nagyrapolt, Albert	1893-	Hungarian. Nobel laureate in biochemistry (1937) for discoveries in biological combustion processes
Havaty, Vaclav	1894-	Czech. Mathematician. Solved mathematical equations to support Einstein's unified field theory
Szilard, Leo	1898-1964 }	Hungarian-born physicists. All played major roles in the development of the atomic bomb. Teller is known as the "father of the hydrogen bomb"
Wigner, Paul	1902- }	
Von Neumann, John	1903-1957 }	
Teller, Edward	1908- }	

Credits

The sources for the illustrations in this book appear below. Credits for pictures from left to right are separated by commas, from top to bottom by dashes.

Cover—Elliott Erwitt from Magnum

8—Elliott Erwitt from Magnum

11—Map by Rafael Palacios

15 through 27—Elliott Erwitt from Magnum

30—Map by Rafael Palacios

32—Culver Pictures, Inc.

35 through 46—Elliott Erwitt from Magnum

49—Map by Rafael Palacios

50, 51—The Bettmann Archive, Culver Pictures, Inc.

56 through 62—Elliott Erwitt from Magnum

63, 64, 65—© 1953 Karsh, Ottawa

66—Elliott Erwitt from Magnum

77—Brown Brothers, United Press International—Underwood and Underwood

78—United Press International— Margaret Bourke-White for FORTUNE

79—U.S. Army Official Photo— Wide World Photos

80—Sovfoto—Wide World Photos

81—Alfred Eisenstaedt, Czecho- press—United Press International

82, 83—Elliott Erwitt from Magnum

84, 85—F. Göess

89 through 97—Elliott Erwitt from Magnum

98, 99—Paul Moor

105—Drawing by Matt Greene

108 through 116—Elliott Erwitt from Magnum

123 through 131—Elliott Erwitt from Magnum

132, 133—Michael Rougier

141 through 148—Elliott Erwitt from Magnum

154 through 160—Elliott Erwitt from Magnum

165, 166, 167—Elliott Erwitt from Magnum

ACKNOWLEDGMENTS

The editors wish to express their appreciation to Dr. M. K. Dziewanowski, Professor of Russian and East European History, Boston University, and Associate, Russian Research Center, Harvard University, who read and commented in detail on the entire text, and who provided especially helpful guidance on historical, political and economic affairs. Valuable help was also provided by Dr. Pavel Korbel, chief consultant on Czechoslovak affairs to the Publications and Special Projects Division of the Free Europe Committee.

Index

This symbol in front of a page number indicates a photograph or painting of the subject mentioned.

Production staff for Time Incorporated

John L. Hallenbeck (Vice President and Director of Production)

Robert E. Foy, James P. Menton, Caroline Ferri and Robert E. Fraser

Text photocomposed under the direction of

Albert J. Dunn and Arthur J. Dunn

x

Printed by R. R. Donnelley & Sons Company, Crawfordsville, Indiana

and The Safran Printing Company, Detroit, Michigan

Bound by R. R. Donnelley & Sons Company, Crawfordsville, Indiana

Paper by The Mead Corporation, Dayton, Ohio

Cover stock by The Plastic Coating Corporation, Holyoke, Massachusetts

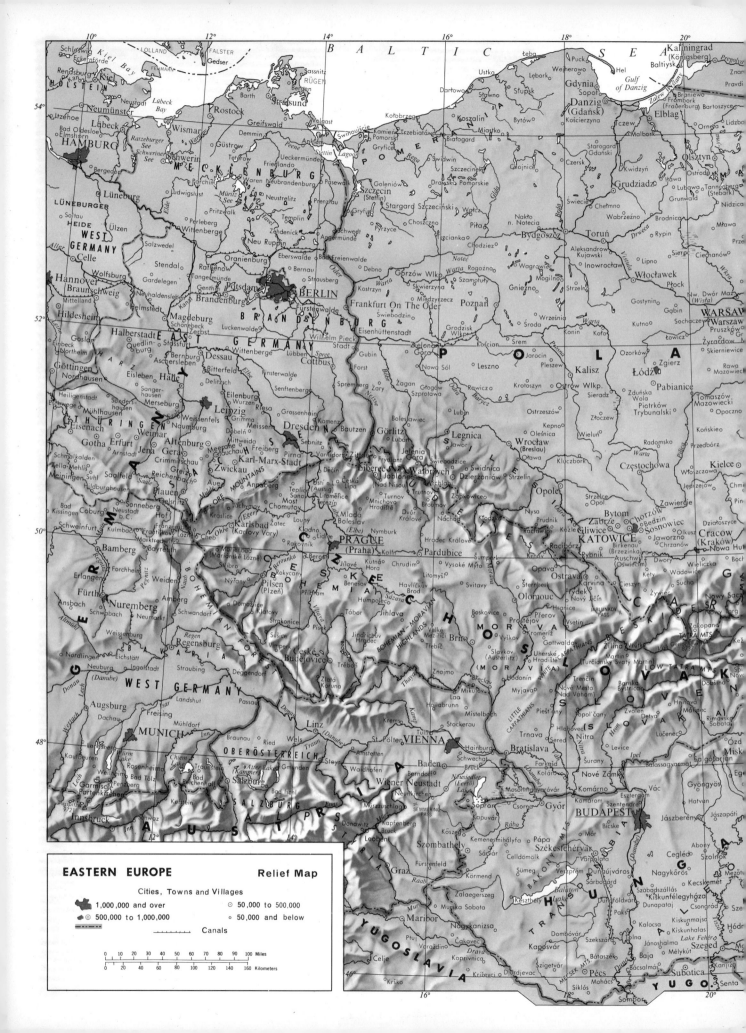

EASTERN EUROPE   Relief Map

Cities, Towns and Villages

1,000,000 and over   ◎ 50,000 to 500,000

500,000 to 1,000,000   ○ 50,000 and below

‑‑‑‑‑   Canals

0 10 20 30 40 50 60 70 80 90 100 Miles

0 20 40 60 80 100 120 140 160 Kilometers